Fearless Parenting

Stepping into Life's Greatest Role Using the Nurtured Heart Approach®

D0752436

Tammy (Small) Fisher, M.Ed.

Fearless Parenting

Stepping into Life's Greatest Role with the Nurtured Heart Approach®

For information contact:

NurturedHeart.net
7132 134th CT SE
Newcastle, WA 98059
tammyfsmall@gmail.com
www.nurturedheart.net

Cover photography provided with permission by 123rf.com, cover design and book formatting by Stephen Huson; copyediting by Dena Klingler; proof copy by Gabriella West at EditforIndies.com. Approved by Howard Glasser.

Printed by Createspace.com

Library of Congress Card Catalog Number: Pending

ISBN 978-0615759524 (Nurturedheart.net)

Printed in the United States
First Printing: March 2013

What others have said about *Fearless Parenting* and Tammy's work

"A powerhouse of compassion and wisdom, Tammy gets right to the essence of being a parent. She helps us all be bolder and more confident in raising our children with joy and love. "

- Tom Grove, M.S.W., parent and author of *The Inner Wealth Initiative: The Nurtured Heart Approach for Educators*

"This book is must read for anyone who is feeling frustrated and overwhelmed in his/her role as a parent. Through Tammy's inspiring stories, humorous and relaxed style of writing, you will come to realize that the very greatness that you wish to instill in your children already exists within; soon you will discover that it is already within you, too."

- Sylvia Miller, wife, mother of nine children ages 3-17 and co-author of *BraveHeart Women: Purpose and Prosperity Revealed Vol. 2*

"Tammy Fisher (Small) is a force of positive energy. Her expertise as a counselor, educator, and parent coach provide a solid framework for her text. She offers a new lens on how parenting can build both the capacity of the adult and the child making the 'the most difficult job on the planet' much more doable for all."

- Dr. Susan Zola, Assistant Superintendent for Achievement, Curriculum and Instruction, Champaign, Illinois. Parent, wife, Greatness Seeker

"What an exceptional mom. Simply brilliant!"

- Tammy's adolescent daughter (nurtured to write this endorsement)

Dedicated to every parent fearlessly holding this book.

ABOUT THE AUTHOR:

An educator for over 30 years, Tammy has worked at all grade levels as teacher, coach, and school counselor. Currently, she thrives as the counselor and NHA coach in a K-8 school, where she teaches students daily and coordinates a Golden Apple®–winning Peer Mediation program. Tammy trains schools across the state and speaks nationally to educators and parents on implementing the Nurtured Heart Approach (www.nurturedheart.net). She holds her B.A. from Western Washington University (1984) where she was nominated Outstanding Elementary School graduate, her Masters from the University of Washington (1995), as well as a Writer's Certificate (2000) and a Certificate in Child and Adolescent Mental Health (2005) from the same university. Tammy lives with her husband in the Seattle area, is a mom of two vibrantly dynamic young adult daughters, Maddison and Braeden – and one easy-to-nurture Wheaten Terrier, Bear.

ACKNOWLEDGEMENTS:

In 2007, based on a grant, I earned the opportunity to become a Certified Nurtured Heart Trainer, working for a full, intense week with creator Howard Glasser and his small crew of gifted Advanced Trainers. Howie's contagious passion lit my spirit on fire and propelled the already strong work I did with students, teachers and parents into a clear realm of transformation. I owe a debt to his generosity, support of all my trainings and acceptance of the adaptations I have made as I work in the trenches with the Nurtured Heart Approach. Additionally, I want to thank the supportive network of Advanced Trainers who live by example, reset genuinely and parent fearlessly. This "go-to" community, both locally and nationally, makes each day a celebration in what is going right. Throughout this book, I cite many other gifted and inspirational educators and innovators in the field of youth development and parent empowerment. Collectively, they have scaffolded the work I do as a Nurtured Heart coach significantly. I must deeply honor the myriad of parents who trusted in NHA and in my conviction that they were already successful. Their stories and indomitable spirits inspired this book.

I wish to thank my mom, Dena Klingler, a former award-winning teacher herself, who relentlessly supported all the decisions in my life, even when they challenged her. Her gift of deep, abiding love of relationship, resiliency and humor was my example as a parent educator – and a parent. My daughters, Maddison and Braeden, were fodder for my stumbling steps as a Nurtured Heart mom and were the perfect humbling reset and celebration of their own sure footing into a confident, independent world. I am so proud of who they are and what they have fearlessly overcome.

Finally, I want to thank my always present and supportive husband, Steve Huson, for his certain faith in the person I have always been and in my mission to write this book (and the last one – and perhaps the next!). His skill with formatting and trouble-shooting made him the poster child for patient spouse and runner-up for sainthood. Blessed and blessings to walk this life with him.

Fearless Parenting:

Stepping into Life's Greatest Role Using the Nurtured Heart Approach

By: Tammy (Small) Fisher, M.Ed.

Table of Contents

Optimism 101:
You Gotta Have Faith

I first began teaching in 1984. Fresh out of college and eager to work with erratically hormonal middle school students, I took a job in a mid-sized town outside of Seattle. Confident and able to look at my perceived failings with a deep sense of humor, I felt prepared to tackle the most challenging child. Of course, in my mind, this child wanted to be at school, wanted to learn, wanted whatever I had to share. I think about my younger self (including that huge perm hairstyle), and I still smile at my own resiliency in responding to difficult, discouraged youth. Optimism. It is one powerful drug in a challenging time. Can it be taught? Can it be fed into the spirits of discouraged learners? The funny thing about me is that I never thought otherwise. I was challenged. Yes. I had rules – and I kept to them (most of the time), but even in response to my most relentlessly Negative Mental Attitude child or parent, I was unable to break my absolute certainty that he/she was capable of every task he/she was given.

Long before I became a school counselor and later met Howard Glasser, creator of The Nurtured Heart Approach®, I had begun to understand how one could establish such a powerful system of relationship. It is logical that in the dynamics of relationship you would always get more of what you name. It is clear that everyone wants to belong. Everyone wants to be seen, be validated. Everyone wants relationship, even negative ones, if that is all they have managed to nurture, because human nature screams for connection. Additionally, positive recognition (meaningful, genuine, positive recognition) goes the distance in increasing the engagement and capacity of my students. Criticism? Not so much.

In 2010, I co-wrote *There's Always Something Going Right: Workbook for Implementing the Nurtured Heart Approach in School Settings* with Louisa Triandis, another great Advanced Trainer, who lived two states away in Southern California. Our goal was to place Glasser's concepts into a usable tool with forms and activities for educators to bring into their classrooms, playgrounds and school policies. Meanwhile, I continued to work in an ethnically, economically diverse K-8 Catholic school, writing columns for parents, leading groups and teaching classes.

Infusing a belief in each person's greatness is my intention. But to a layperson not versed in the Nurtured Heart Approach, this can sound a bit fluffy and simple. Greatness? Really. What about math? What about social studies? Verb conjugation? And isn't all this self-esteem stuff a bit much? "The problem is kids lack work ethic." "Kids get everything handed to them." "Kids are entitled and disrespectful." Sound like any adults you know?

I am not saying it is easy being an optimist. But it sure beats the alternative. When I do school trainings, I often point out that there is a good reason I didn't name my last book: *Well, It Could Be Worse.* Hard times are certain (like taxes, right?). But the piece of the puzzle that remains mine to own is this: ATTITUDE. Attitude is choice. Events may not be. Things may sometimes, if I may quote the word forbidden in my school, "suck!" But how we respond is definitely a choice. I teach my students daily that they are 100 percent responsible for every word out of their mouths and 100 percent responsible for every action. You cannot control others. You cannot control the world. But your attitude? Yes! That is yours to own. What a powerful concept to give to a child. He/she gets to choose optimism. Something is always going right.

Perhaps I am hard-wired this way. I had my share of childhood trauma over which I had no control. But this piece of me, this optimism, is my ultimate faith in myself, as well as an optimistic faith in others' intentions, and is at the core of how I view and interact in my world. All people are good. They just sometimes need to be "reset" to their greatness. They simply forget/forgot their greatness. And sometimes we forget our own when we let a child drag us down to a space of negative energy and complaints.

This may explain why I do the work I do: Kids are great. Not just a few. All kids. As I work in partnership to support the work of Rick Miller, the founder, and Wally Endicott, the Executive Director, of *Kids At Hope*™ in the Northwest, I align solidly with the *Kids At Hope*™ belief statement: *All Kids Are Capable of Success: NO EXCEPTIONS!*

This series of chapters and musings over the challenges to stepping into life's greatest role as a parent is designed to build on the initial work of Howard Glasser in his creation of The Nurtured Heart Approach. Taking the core concepts and expanding them into my own work as a parent of two teenage daughters, parent coach, educator working with parents, and a Nurtured Heart Advanced Trainer, I try to address the common themes that come up in my parent groups or conversations with parents in my work and personal world. I have elicited insight from other NHA trainers, Howie and my own children (who often reply to me with a smirk when I go out of my way to name greatness in one of their choices: "Nice Nurtured Heart, Mom"). I know, deep down, they appreciate the recognition. But then, I am an optimist, after all.

(Note to reader: This author will reference the Nurtured Heart Approach throughout, knowing it has been registered. NHA is an abbreviation of this and all non-NHA concepts will be identified as such, though all are included as compatible supports to NHA constructs in building capacity and greatness in our children. For more formal information on Nurtured Heart Approach, coaching, resources, and training, visit ChildrensSuccessFoundation.com.)

P.ositive M.ental A.ttitude 101:

An Abstract of the Nurtured Heart Approach

I was a mediocre (generous analysis at best) basketball player from elementary school right through my senior year in high school. When I became a junior high teacher (something I far excelled at in comparison), I signed on to be the assistant girls' basketball coach. Taking the lead from the dynamic head coach, Wendy, I learned to holler like the best of them: "How's your P.M.A.?" We would erupt like drill sergeants. "Boy, am I ENTHUSIASTIC!" would be the required reply. Simply recalling the energy of youth, the compliance, the eagerness to learn and be challenged, I was definitely enthusiastic – pretty much the poster child of Enthusiastic. (You can't play ball for that many years and not have some recognition of your lack of a successful jump shot.) Having a **P**ositive **M**ental **A**ttitude went way beyond the challenges of running lines in practice for the girls. It was what kept them coming to practice, even during our losing season, and it was what brought them back the next year to make it to the finals.

The Nurtured Heart Approach is P.M.A. (Positive Mental Attitude) at its core. It is not, however, simply a fluffy system that encourages false self-esteem. It IS all about realistic capability. It IS all about where you, as a significant adult in the life of a child, put your energy in that relationship. And finally, it IS all about directing that positive energy toward maintaining high and consistent expectations. Initially, Howard Glasser illustrated this concept by using the model of a three-legged stool or table. Without one of the legs, the stool (the child, our relationship, and all our great intentions) will tip over and be ineffective. More recently, in his newest book *Notching Up the Nurtured Heart Approach: The New Inner Wealth Initiative for Educators* (Glasser and Block, 2011), Glasser tells the adult to consider the three constructs as Stands which an adult takes in relationship. They are firm, consistent ways of being in relationship that build capacity for children (and even for anyone in our lives when we apply them). The clarity and logic of the Stands become obvious as you connect them to the energetic relationship you have with your children. While I assume that many of my readers are familiar with Howard Glasser's Nurtured Heart Approach, and have read one or more of his books, or mine for educators, I give here a very basic overview of the three core constructs/Stands[1] which are expanded in detail throughout the chapters and articles ahead:

---

[1] A list of several of the books referenced above can be found in the appendix. This author highly suggests reading one of these completely, in addition to the essays included here, as all are based and referenced throughout this parent resource.

1. Refuse to Energize Negativity: "Absolutely No!"

2. Relentlessly Energize the Positive: "Absolutely Yes!"

3. Clearly Enforce the Limits (knowing your child is capable of following every given rule): "Absolute Clarity!"

While each of these Stands, in and of itself, is an excellent direction in relationship, it is truly only when we employ all three with consistency that we will see transformation in relationship. Glasser and Block state this most clearly when they use the analogy of juggling three balls.

> *"Most people can juggle one ball right away. Most can juggle two within a few minutes. But nobody picks up three balls and starts juggling the first time trying, no matter how athletically gifted he or she might be. In learning and applying the Nurtured Heart Approach, there will be three 'balls' you'll learn to juggle by getting them in the air one at a time....If you don't get the first two balls in the air before adding the third, the approach will not work."*[2]

Howard Glasser calls this commitment to being a full-on Nurtured Heart parent "Taking A Stand." Take a Stand with your child and REFUSE TO GIVE ANY NEGATIVE ENERGY TO BROKEN RULES. Drop the anger, drop the warnings, and drop the heightened relationship when things are going wrong. You will not go to that place of triggered negativity

---

[2] Glasser and Block, c. 2011 p. 39

any more: Absolute No! Take a Stand with your child and ALWAYS NAME AND SEE GREATNESS: Absolute Yes! Even when your child is challenging, use a lens that works to see there is always something going right. And finally, Take a Stand and ALWAYS UPHOLD/MAINTAIN YOUR LIMITS/RULES: Absolute Clarity! Many parents and others working with children want to begin with this last Stand, so as we explore this approach as it relates to consequences, it is critical that you hold onto the example from Glasser's book: Don't toss this last "ball" (Stand) into your parent juggling trick until you are firmly successful with those first two "balls" (Stands). Begin with your Stand of Absolute No! to negativity and Absolute Yes! to seeing greatness. And as with any transformative idea, as you work toward fluency and authenticity, you must start with using these same Stands with yourself. It is hard to hold the mirror up to your child and name the greatness you see if you shy away from staring into the greatness that is you.

Glasser highlights the critical need to not wait for your children to be good. See them as good right now. Set them up for success, by "hijacking" them (his term) into the next great choice. In the same way you place gates around stairs to keep toddlers from tumbling and training wheels on bikes to encourage the first steps toward independence, the wise adult creates opportunities for your children's successful mastery with a thoughtful structure that provides numerous chances for the children to be seen and named for making good choices (sometimes right before they are about to make a poor one). A hijacked moment is one where the adult does just that: names a great choice to promote a great choice. Your energy in that moment can set children up to repeat great choices – or continue down a path where you simply remove your relationship to the bad choice, consequence it cleanly and set them up for a rapid, upcoming moment to try again or "reset." In the chapters that follow, examples of these ideas and concepts will be flushed out in greater detail. We will tackle each of these Stands/Legs of the Stool in reference to specific issues which arise as each parent "bellies up to the bar of greatness" in his/her own parenting style. You are as unique and as complex as your child. The approach will never fail if you believe in your own capability to handle anything that comes your way. This is what you MUST believe for your own children's capability to be successful. So do not falter in this conviction for yourself. Know it. Name it. Take a deep Stand for it. Relentless Positive Mental Attitude is MUST for the greatness of you as you bring out greatness in your children. If you begin by believing in your own greatness, it is a simple step to being entrenched in the certainty of this for your children.

The Parent Trap:
Resetting Yourself as an Amazing, if Not Perfect, Parent

Inevitably, as I introduce the Nurtured Heart Approach™ to parents, they quickly go to self-blame and criticism ias to how they may have parented in the past. But just as you will coach your children to let go of past mistakes and move toward all the great choices they are now making, you must model the same. A father of three became very silent after I had introduced the core ideas of NHA to him and his wife. After each sharing aloud how they saw the greatness of each family member present, he became close to tears. When I asked him what he was thinking, he smiled ruefully, "I feel like I have really messed up. Nobody teaches you this stuff. But it makes so much sense. Everyone should learn this. Where was this in my schooling? I took all kinds of classes (as a physician) but nothing as useful as this." That sort of aha moment is a common reaction among Nurtured Heart converts and practitioners. And I suppose that is why it resonates with so many of us. But replaying the tapes of our parenting faux pas will not make us greater parents. It sucks the positive energy and intention out of us when we focus on failure. So as you work to bring out the best version of your children, you need to recognize the power of this P.M.A. in regards to you as a parent. The Ghost of Parent Past we can learn from, squirm from, and move from. But why pal around with him? Glasser calls this a RESET when we time ourselves out. It is a simple, quick emotionless reminder that we slipped from our greatness and now we are welcomed back. Model this for your kids. Make it a quick "Whoops!" and then get back to your intentional P.M.A. and the next opportunity to show your greatness.

Another parent, challenged by this idea and trying so hard to see how positive recognition must come before energy to negative choices, debated with me: "But how can I learn from my past mistake if I don't focus on it?" Delightful question. Focusing on something implies a lens that zooms in, giving deep analysis and energy to the problem. I simply don't think you need to do that to learn that that past choice didn't work. To ruminate on it? To wish it different? To parent-police after the fact seems to be energy in the wrong direction. So you messed up. Reset back to greatness. Let your kids know you forgot how great you were for a minute, and how great they were. Now you are back (to your Greatness Pedestal, I like to say). Focusing on the past will not make your kids greater kids either. But energizing the success you have <u>now</u> will! The greatness of this flip is recognizing you can do it better next time. Isn't that what you want for your kids, too?

In jest, a friend of mine likes to say that if your child makes it to 18 alive and not in prison, you did pretty well as a parent. Of course, most of us have big dreams and intentions for our kids. When they falter or struggle, we bear a deep angst, sometimes unspoken. Could this be the fatal error in judgment that starts the ball rolling toward homelessness, high school drop out, drug addiction, unemployment, and failed relationships? While I exaggerate greatly, my nearly 30 years of working with parents upholds this wobbly concept that our children are a few steps away from disaster if we don't intervene. Seems like a lot of energy to negativity to me and also not very empowering to our kids. That way of thinking implies that we don't see them as capable of handling all life's challenges. So we start there. We start with their capabilities and then our own capability to scaffold our children with the Stands of the approach: 1) Absolute No negative energy; 2) Absolute Yes to full focus on successes; 3) Absolute Clarity in regards to limits. Consider yourself reset to your Greatness Pedestal, and now let's strategize some ways to introduce your new parenting approach to your family.

> *WAIT, WAIT, WAIT... What about consequences?? It sounds good enough on paper, all this positive recognition and naming what is going right, but my kid talks back, my kid won't do his chores, my kid is late for curfew, my kid lies about his homework, my kid kicks his little sister... And so on...*

Sound familiar? Nearly each time I begin to work with a family at my school, in parent groups, or in their homes, they desire to jump right to the consequences. It is often the main reason that they seek a parent coach or a therapist to "fix" their child. They have reached a level of panic (see examples above) and a perceived crisis. Even the moment is a clear indicator that they gotta get some P.M.A. <u>now</u>. Out of the habit of seeing the mistakes their kids are making, they have overlooked all the times the child WAS honest, <u>didn't</u> hit his sister, <u>followed</u> a direction the first time, or <u>came home</u> on time. Getting parents to slow down and recognize why beginning with a stand on consequences will only backfire without the other Stands intact is the critical first step.

Be patient. Your child wasn't born breaking rules, and they certainly fell hundreds of times as they were learning to walk. Though I bet they walk quite normally now, right? Taking the risk to shift the lens to only what is going right feels unstable and scary. "Should I not consequence a broken rule?" they often ask. Certainly, just be sure you are looking for all the times the rules aren't broken! We will focus more on this in our chapter on Mom Needs a Time-Out. Meanwhile, be patient.

Parents are made, not born.

Introducing NHA to Your Family: Simple Suggestions for Success as a Fearless Parent

While I am not a big fan of focusing on the past errors of our ways, I am a fan of admitting we could have done it differently. Often this candor is refreshing to family members who have waged battle zones for a while. You know your kids best and your voice has to be authentically yours, but I recommend possibly scripting this new direction to help you frame it successfully. This dry-run version can solidify your conviction in the power of energizing what is going right again and again and again. It can be so addictive to recognize good choices, self-control, resiliency, acceptance of responsibility, teamwork, patience, cooperation, respect – and more patience, yet again. Calling the family meeting and beginning with a statement that acknowledges some of your stumbling blocks reflects your greatness to move past the past. It also allows the same for your family members. Clean slate = new sheriff in town!

Here, I provide a lengthy introduction of how you might open up this parenting paradigm shift. Your own voice, understanding of your own desired outcomes, and the developmental age of your children are factors in creating a realistic conversation. As an additional suggestion, I would say less is more, here. So choosing to really demonstrate your intention to be positive OR your goal to be less angry or negative might be a simple first conversation. This example incorporates both to simply illustrate the conversations possible.

"As I continue to learn more as a parent, I realize I have unintentionally missed some great moments to support your good choices. You make all kinds of good choices all day long and so often you ARE following the rules and the simple requests we make of you. In fact, you do this more than not! It's amazing what a supportive member of this family you are becoming. I am proud of your growing maturity and the steps you are taking to become independent and responsible. Unfortunately, I have been paying attention at the wrong moments quite a bit. Complaining to you about unfinished chores, nagging at you to do something that you already know

you need to do. I have even done things for you that you are so capable of doing for yourself. Wow! I realize now that this hasn't helped build your greatness at all. In fact, it has done more the opposite. It has made you think that sometimes you aren't capable of following all our rules and directions. Are you capable of _____? (Name a specific task that your child(ren) are required to do.) *I see nodding – of course! Our naggings and warnings have let you believe that you need help all the time. Instead of building up your skills and noticing all your successful choices, we sometimes give you warnings as though you are not able to do something the first time. ...."*

If your energy and tone is sincere and not sarcastic, this speech should feel like validation to your child. "Of course I am capable! It's about time you noticed!" Here is where you can "hijack" your children toward the best version of themselves. Name a few examples of times where they followed rules easily. Add words that describe what these skills say about them as leaders and how these behaviors make you feel about their capabilities.

"Just yesterday, Kyle, you got up right when your alarm went off. Did I stop and tell you how that mature, responsible behavior just made my morning? (He likely shakes his head and remembers you may have simply given him a command about his next needed step.) *That is what I mean about you making great choices. I am going to notice these more often. And you will earn your privileges and opportunities based on your doing these*

things and following our rules – even when you would rather not! Even earlier in the week when I asked you to take the recycling bins in from the front, you didn't do it right away and I reminded you. It made us both very grumpy, and what I know now is that you don't need me to remind you, do you? You know what you need to do. I need to trust in you more, because you also know that if you have done your chores by dinnertime, you earn your computer time. That rule hasn't changed – and yet I talk to you like you need reminding. You can handle it if you don't get your computer time. It is your choice at that point. I am so sorry for not treating you as a growing, responsible member of our family, honoring our rules and staying firm with them..."

"Wait! Are you telling me he can still choose not to do the chore?" a panicked parent responds. Yep. In fact, he can break all the rules. The key is that you are going to reward him with all the privileges, relationships, and recognition when he CHOOSES to follow the family rules. Be transparent, here. Let him know you are going to be looking to name his successful choices, including participating in the family meeting. Let him know, too, that you know he does things he doesn't want to do because it helps the family or is part of becoming a responsible student. You are going to work to notice more of that all the time. You can continue to lay out the new ground rules – including the "rules" you are going to work on for yourself (no nagging, warnings, yelling, etc.). Involve family members in coming up with both their responsibilities AND the rewards. The rewards ARE the consequence for following up with the responsibilities and expectations.

This is a great time to introduce them to the Nurtured Heart Approach version of a time-out (reset). It is very critical that they see this as an opportunity to restart – and not a punishment. It is equally important that you, as a parent, deliver it as such, without anger or rancor, blame or resentment.

> *"As this is a new way for me to parent with you, it will take me a while to break some bad habits. When I slip up, I am going to 'reset' myself back to Mom-the-Great by stepping away, taking some deep breaths and refocusing. It is like the time-outs we would give you when we sent you to your room if you talked back to us. I know when you talk back you are just frustrated and need to calm down, too. Now you can 'reset' right where you are. You can simply just sit on a chair or stool or even the stairs and close your eyes for a minute and when you are ready to try being timed-in again, you are welcomed back.*
>
> *Now, instead of myself or your father lecturing you on why you got the time-out, we are just going to welcome you back. Instead of me scolding you or yelling back, I will ask you to "reset" and I will reset myself, too. The quicker you give us the reset, the more quickly you get back to all the great privileges of a timed-in life. Friends, Buster, your dog, television, and computer time you may have earned, and so on. We won't take any of that from*

> *you; you just have to be timed-in to our family to enjoy them."*

Consider eliciting more buy-in from your family by having them brainstorm words or phrases the family may use to signal a "reset." In my earlier book, I shared one that clicked for me and some of my families: "sideline." As so many of my families have kids that play or watch sports, this one resonated familiarity. If you are on the sideline, you are not in the game. Being in the game is where you want to be. Being in the game is where all the privileges and relationships of life exist. "Take a sideline" was how one dad said they called for their son to "reset." Again, the key is to remain calm, to say it just once and expect compliance, and to remember to give it no extra relationship. It is also important to remind your child that a "sideline," "take five," "give me a minute," or "press pause" is an opportunity for the child, and ourselves, to get back on track and get back in the game. It is a breather of sorts, which actually allows quick redemption. Unlike former time-outs, which could drag out meaninglessly and create resentment, a true reset (because it is not punishment, but simply a quick removal of our positive relationship), should build capacity and responsibility each time a child accepts the reset. Welcome him back into the game as soon as you can, and quickly look for a way to energize his good choices, even his ability to accept the reset and try again!

Once you have established a family word or phrase for "reset," you can good-naturedly role-play a situation where a reset would be appropriate. If both parents are involved, you can demonstrate what it might look like both to be reset and to be welcomed back. If just one parent is presenting the concept, you talk it through first and then let the child give the parent a "practice" reset, so you can show them what you want them to do.

Here is a way I explained the idea of resets to an intense student in my school:

"It is not punishment, remember; it is just a way for you to calm down before you possibly make a situation worse. Sometimes you can reset yourself in a few seconds, sometimes you may need to go sit on the stair or in another room to get yourself 'reset' and ready to get back into the game. Our goal is that eventually those longer resets turn into quick ones, and you are in the game nearly all the time.

"Think about a friend of yours at recess who gets all upset because someone said he was tagged out and he didn't think he was. At that moment, if he can stop himself and reset, he might have a positive outcome. Maybe people will listen to him. Maybe they will let him do it again. Maybe he will simply accept that it doesn't matter. Maybe he will realize it is just a game at recess. But if he is too emotional and intense and doesn't reset, his friends can decide they don't want to play with him. He can lose his temper and hit someone. He can get in trouble. He can make it worse. A reset is a way to keep you from making a situation worse, to help you become

more self-aware, and to help you get back in the game as a team player that everyone wants on their team."

Isn't that what we are seeking as we parent our kids: To give our children the skills to handle anything that comes their way with confidence and self-awareness? Who wouldn't want to be on that kid's team?

Shifting Away from Negativity:
Arguing, Complaining, and Blaming

I was recently reading a delightful memoir by Rhoda Jantzen[3]. In the midst of healing from much loss, she considers the idea of virtue and virtuous people. In a rich and humorous way, she elaborates the concept that virtue is really a choice. It is not something some people are born with – and others lack. Arguably, it can be nurtured because, as the saying goes, virtue is its own reward. As I reread the interesting passage, I considered the parallel to focusing on negativity and negative choices.

An example of this mind-frame is exhibited in a story that was shared with me and paraphrased here:

"Within the Babemba tribe in South Africa, antisocial or criminal behavior is infrequent, but when it does occur, the tribe has an interesting ritual for dealing with it.

If a member of the tribe acts irresponsibly, he is placed in the center of the village. Work stops and every man, woman and child gather around the accused, forming a

3 *Mennonite in a Little Black Dress: A Memoir of Going Home* by Rhoda Jantzen (c. 2010)

large circle. Then, one at a time, each individual, including the children, call out all the good things the person in the center has done in his lifetime.

All his positive attributes, good deeds, strengths and kind acts are recited carefully and at length. No one is permitted to tell an untruth, to exaggerate or to be facetious. The ceremony often lasts for several days and doesn't stop until everyone is drained of every positive comment he or she can muster about the person within the circle. Not a word of criticism about him or his irresponsible, antisocial behavior is permitted. At the end, the tribal circle breaks up, a joyous celebration begins, and the person is welcomed back into the tribe."[4]

Whether this amazing tribe exists or behaves as stated, even the retelling of the story speaks to a core in our being that looks toward what is going right, that looks toward redemption and away from criticism. What we are doing right has far more power to transform than what we ever do wrong. This is hard-wired in our brains. We can both feed our greatness and feed those with whom we connect, or we will end up minimized and defined by our errors. History should serve us as a lesson, not as a definition of our future.

---

[4] *Sower's Seeds of Encouragement: Fifth Planting 100 Stories of Hope, Humor and Healing* by Brian Cavanaugh (c. 1998)

The shift in the Nurtured Heart Approach to this critical view must be direct and intentional. The first step to change is awareness. Try this exercise:

Enter the room where your child is playing / working / gaming / texting / watching TV, etc. (p.s. anything but focusing on you!) Observe. Look at the room. Look at the intensity of your child's focus. Name five things that are going right. Push yourself to say them aloud if you can. "I see you focused. I see you persisting. I see you playing independently and making independent choices. I see you managing your time well. I see you making creative choices. I see you working out problems. I can almost hear your brain thinking, you are so engaged."

Imagine, conversely, that you have asked your children to come to the table for dinner. You have asked them to put away their dirty clothes. You have told them they had just five minutes left on the game / TV / texting, etc. They have failed to do any of these simple requests. Again. Your mind slips right to the habit of criticism. They are breaking these rules to make you mad. They are irresponsible and immature. Why can't they do these without nagging? Do they like when you nag? Do they like to have more privileges removed? Blah, blah, blah... the mind so quickly can shift, can't it? This is where the real challenge of not energizing negativity comes to play. The Nurtured Heart Approach reminds us that relationship is relationship. Nagging is relationship. We hate nagging, right? So what if we stopped? "They wouldn't do what we asked." Really? Remember all life's privileges are tied to their capabilities to handle the rules. I challenge you to consider that part of the reason they don't do what we ask the first time, is because they like the relationship, despite its negative energy. It works for them.

After self-awareness, the second step of this clarity is to begin to understand that if we respond to behavior with energy, we get more of that behavior. Nagging actually draws out the action. Reminding becomes a dance of "how many times must I..." Well, at least this time, I guess. With NHA, you are called to step off the dance floor.

When I first began using the Nurtured Heart Approach with my own children, I slipped off my greatness pedestal most of the time. In fact, getting clean NHA is initially much more challenging with your own offspring, by the way, than it is this with anyone else's children. I may suggest that if you are feeling discouraged with your inability to stay clean of negative energizing, and want some reinforcement to your greatness and intention, go hang out with your friend's kids and enjoy how easy it is to see, name and honor greatness, as well as step away from paying any attention to negative behavior. Remember, we are our children's favorite toys! They have the wind-up button – but now, you are learning the rewind knob yourself!

The essential element of diffusing negativity is to simply not respond. Yep. Okay, there we go. That's it. End of chapter. Next?

Oh? Sounds simple, but I recognize, from my own wiring, that not responding is not easy. I hate whining. My kids have so much. Why must they whine when my request is so small? Why must they complain all the time? I didn't complain when I was a kid (well, hardly). And why can't they do anything I ask of them without arguing or yelling?

Why? Because, in reality, this is actually a part of growing up. As researchers explore the personalities of adults who harbor the shortest fuses, and quick tempers, it is being revealed that children of authoritarian, versus authoritative parents, were not allowed a voice. This very strictness to rules, which Glasser outlines as a core construct in the Nurtured Heart Approach, has always been a part of an authoritarian household. However, here, there is also much relationship to negativity and very little recognition of the positive. The authoritarians are the boss. They are the "Because I said so" response to the why.[5] They have strict rules. They often threaten, spank or use other corporal punishment to establish this authority and compliance. It actually often works in that moment, too.

But the fallout in this power dichotomy is the children's inner wealth and the development of their own sense of individual greatness and power. The children are rarely recognized for what they do well, and while they learn (or suffer punishment) to follow the rules, it does not come from a place of capability, but from fear. The loss of voice in the child creates an angry or complacent child who can harbor

---

[5] See activity in Chapter 9 on *Creative Strategies,* which directly addresses this response.

this attitude against authority, can feel marginalized by adults – and then grow up to repeat the cycle.

In contrast to the authoritarian, a permissive parent has got the positive energy down, but lacks consistency to his/her rules. So yet again the children do not learn how capable they are of following life's boundaries. The permissive parent's negative energy is made of more of warnings, "next times," and pleas for compliance. Here children learn their voices have power and impact, while the adults struggle with boundaries, expectations, and realistic goals. Permissive parents, with great intention and love, want to save their children from pain or struggles, want to make life easier, want to be their children's friend. We don't need to do a benefit analysis on this parenting style to see the resulting adult brought up in a world where behavior boundaries were inconsistent, and a child's capability was not earned and rewarded with the building of his/her inner wealth.

Alternatively, the authoritative parent remains the "boss" of wisdom, but doesn't need to bully to teach a child how to cope with his or her world, nor ignore rules out of fear that the child can't handle them. The authoritative parent is also Strictness to Rules; however, this parent recognizes that a child <u>must</u> push boundaries and test limits in the safety of that relationship in order to grow and learn how to handle all life's challenges. The authoritative parent can handle that push, even when it makes them uncomfortable or disappointed. It is the Fearless Parent's persistence and conviction that develops the child's ability to navigate the challenges of his or her world.

<u>Accept this</u>: Children will complain. Children will argue. Children will fight with their siblings. Children will whine. Children will fail to follow through. And most importantly: It is NOT about you, the parent! Phew! What is about you, however, is how you choose to respond. This is a bold model you pass on to your child: we can choose and control our response. Choice implies again that no one can make you do anything. It is a powerful truth (one that I will come back to as we refortify ourselves in Chapter 4 on Strictness to Rules), and it plays well for your ability to step away from an argument, ignore a complaining, whining child, and not give energy to the "talking back" response. In all of these examples, relationship around negativity is pulled away. You may feel the angst. You may sense your own disbelief at their response. But remember, that is your child's job: to test limits. And it is your job, say it with me ☺: to set them. And as I once texted to my ninth grader many years back, when she was doing all of the above: "Guess what? We are both doing our jobs."

What does this really take? The firm Stands of NHA, a belief in your child's ability to handle all of life's expectations, and a belief in your own greatness as a parent bringing this gift of awareness to your child. An argument takes two people to maintain.[6] Without a debate, you simply have a monologue.

Quick: What positive qualities is your child showing when he/she argue? What about when he/she is willing to give a

---

[6] See my essay "An Argument for Arguing" in Chapter 10: *Things That Make You Go Hmm...*

monologue with an entire list of rationales? What does it say when a child is complaining about a duty or a request? Here, we can take a step back to realize that our child is an independent thinker – and independent of us. Our children are working to navigate a world without much personal power. We could easily bully them into doing what we want (especially if we have the keys!); therefore there is a risk involved for children when they argue.

But they do it anyway. They see their world as one of abundance and possibility, options and choices. Not a bad way to see the world, I believe. We see the world this way, too, if we are Nurtured Heart practitioners – or simply glass-half-full professors. We are also smart enough to know that our world has boundaries, that the options are varied, but not without limits and consequences. The balance is the hard part. Appreciate your pushback child. As the significant adult, we need to disengage until he/she calms down. Acknowledge the energy it took the child, the creativity, the focus and persistence. All these are incredible qualities of greatness that are so useful in navigating their world.

The following is a success story to illustrate how this works so well.

Armed with fresh Stands of the Nurtured Heart Approach, the parent brings her five-year-old son, Derek, to the ToysRUs® kids' overload world to purchase a gift for his cousin, who is turning seven. She knows that it will be a battle, bringing her kid into the clutches of the proverbial candy store. Historically, she has been a permissive parent, who then blows after numerous reminders, warnings and finally giving-ins. Armed with the positive potential of NHA, she is up for the challenge. She wants her son to learn to share and give, developmentally a struggle at this age, but not impossible. She also wants to make shopping in general less of a battle zone.

Prior to entering the store, she "hijacks" Derek, Glasser's term for setting him up as great in the middle of an accidental action, by naming what he is doing right: "Derek, look at you being so patient waiting for Mom to get the cart. I can tell you are already thinking about what Joey, your cousin, might want. He is lucky to have you as a cousin." NOTE: Those new practitioners to NHA might have trouble not rolling their eyes at the heavy-handed statements, but the reality of this recognition is that it helps raise the bar for Derek <u>before</u> the challenge even begins. Consider any "battle" you have at home: bedtime, dinnertime, getting up in the morning, picking up after yourself. This system of hijacking is a brilliant tool, which works flawlessly if you keep the warnings, naggings and any negative intention out of your tone. It requires pre-planning and practice, but the payback is that even the parent feels great about her kid when she shares these observations. Derek may push back by starting in on his own list of desires or arguing when pushed to task, but mom can stay firm and ignore his comments completely. She wants a relationship with Derek the Great. She will not give him relationship when he is slipping off that pedestal.

She persists: "Derek, I know you are going to see a lot of fun things here. It is okay to tell me things you like, too. We are just getting Joey his gift today, though, and you have lots of good ideas about what he might like because you know him best." Here we accept that he IS a kid in the candy store, not denying that he will want things and like things. And as Derek names things he likes, mom acknowledges his good taste, his creativity, and his resourcefulness. When he begs, mom turns away. When he bargains, mom does not respond. When Derek tries his full throttle negotiation, mom meets him with full greatness: "You are being so persistent and patient looking for something for your cousin when it is so hard not to want something for yourself, Derek. I am so impressed with your maturity. Even how clever you are to negotiate! You named three things that Joey would like. If you were Joey, which one would you like to open and be surprised at the most?" Distraction, recognition, and most of all Calm Mom who has accepted that she can't take Derek's intensity away, but she can use his creativity to build skills.

But, oh-oh, Derek is now hyper-focused on a toy in his hand. He can't be distracted. Mom of the Past would have admonished Derek, told him he was being selfish, warned irrationally that she wouldn't bring him here again, escalating the conflict by building negativity around the situation. Her increasingly intense child in a public place would have embarrassed Mom of Child Past, especially when he began to hit her leg and raise his voice louder. Mom of Child Past would simply say, "Okay, but just this one thing, Derek. I mean it." BAM! Child of Incapability to Follow Rules would be briefly rewarded and ultimately reinforced: Whining and making a scene works!

Newly Energized Mom of NHA recognizes that Derek is being a reasonable boy, struggling with desire and also really wanting relationship. Mom says, "Hmmmm...." and looks away at another aisle. Derek persists. She persists. The moment he stops the begging, perhaps to try a new approach or take a breath, mom does the full NHA assault to his greatness: "Wow, Derek. I am so impressed with you right now. You really wanted that toy and you were having trouble remembering our deal to get a gift for Joey – and then go to lunch ourselves. You had to work to show such self-control. You calmed yourself down! All on your own. I didn't even tell you to calm down. I can't wait to tell your dad and your auntie how you picked out Joey's toy, even though you wanted one for yourself. Are you sure you aren't the one who is going to be seven instead of Joey?? You are acting like such a big boy."

Okay, eye-rollers unite! While this monologue of greatness may seem over the top or even a challenge to many parents who are habitual "Good job" folks, it works. It really works. There is no condescending tone, no sarcasm or "bullying" into following through. There is simply the truth in the moment, as Glasser coaches. The mom who shared this story in one of my parent groups began quietly to share at first how much she hated taking her son anywhere near a store. In a previous session, I had shared that in order to be calm during the assault of a begging child, we really have to reframe our perspective of the child in the situation. We have to see that we really want our child to want things, to challenge the "order," to look toward abundance. We also want to help children handle the boundaries, accept the "No," and regulate themselves back to calm. This mom took this to heart. She began to see her son's requests as part of his desire to fit into his world, to establish his own identity in a bigger place and to see if boundaries really were firm. That shift motivated her to try the ToysRUs "experiment."

As she elaborated on her adventure with Derek, the whole group was moved emotionally to applaud her relentless parenting. How easy was it for us to energize this mom's risk-taking? We recognized that she picked a most challenging starting point for her new skill and intention. She clearly began to see her son as capable of handling the boundaries, and most importantly, she saw herself as capable of setting them, naming them, upholding them, and supporting Derek's ability throughout it all. I think we all wanted a field trip to ToysRUs that same afternoon.

A Final Caveat on Negativity

Tackling negative people is another challenge as you begin to bring the Nurtured Heart Approach firmly into your relationships. Frequently, parents will complain. (Yes, I get the irony.) His or her spouse, in-law or *own* parent is negative. This other significant adult yells, focusing on their child's mistakes, energizing negativity with every escalated response. One of the most notable responses to becoming a habitual NHA practitioner is a mental shift away from both the negativity and the negative.

My daughter, now 20, works a part-time job with an unhappy co-worker. The young woman is a blanket of complaining – moving about a bit like Pig-Pen in Charlie Brown cartoons, a cloud of dusty negativity surrounding her. It drains my daughter, exhausts her toward avoidance. We all know this person. Using my relentless positive energy, I have really begun to see these people differently. The complaining co-worker, the parent who yells, the criticizing relative – all of these individuals have a common element. They have forgotten their greatness. If, and when, we tap into ours clearly (remember, great, not perfect), it becomes an easy, next step to go out of our way to be gracious to them. We don't need anything in return, but we can give and build capacity. If they complain, just as we would with a complaining child, we do not respond or engage. If they grumble, we can name a quality of greatness in them. "It is so obvious that you care a great deal about your son and his success. He is lucky to have someone who cares so much." My daughter, well versed by her NHA mom, knows to try this. She says, "Have good day!" as Negative Nelly leaves, despite the girl's clear mission otherwise. She goes out of her way to ask the girl questions about herself. She persists, and she doesn't take it personally.

In the same way that we are drawn to positive people and their aura, we can be that kind of pay-it-forward person in the face of deep negativity. Remember, each person is responsible for every word or action he or she creates. Never download Negative Ned or Nelly's comments or attitudes. Additionally, consider being as relentless with Ned as you would be with your own child or spouse. We know, for many Nellys, that their cups are half-full and their life experiences have not taught them to see their own greatness. They will push back, just as a challenged child might, who is used to only getting relationship when things are going wrong. Lucky us. We see the light. We are the light. We can share the light. And on those few days when we find ourselves headed into the darkness, the best reset we can provide for ourselves is to stop and list all the great things about our kids. Our kids (friends, partners, family) are the best toys on the rack. And we get to nurture their greatness daily. Lucky us.

This Cherokee Legend is one I often share to illustrate energy in relationship:

TWO WOLVES

An old Cherokee is teaching his grandson about life. "A fight is going on inside me," he says to the boy. "It is a terrible fight and it is between two wolves. One is evil – he is anger, envy, sorrow, regret, greed, arrogance, self-pity, guilt, resentment, inferiority, lies, false pride, superiority, and ego." He continued, "The other is good – he is joy, peace, love, hope, serenity, humility, kindness, benevolence, empathy, generosity, truth, compassion, and faith. The same fight is going on inside you – and inside every other person."

The grandson thought about it for a minute and then asked his grandfather, "Which wolf will win?"

The old Cherokee simply replied, "The one you feed."[7]

---

[7] This is a classic tale, which appears in many books, websites, and presenter stories. This version was found online at www.firstpeople.us.

Time-Outs:
They're Not Just for Kids Anymore

Game on!

Howard Glasser, when he first formulated the intentional constructs of the Nurtured Heart Approach, recognized the powerful pull of video games. A child engaged in a video game is actually in a kind of relationship that has very rigid boundaries. The rules in the game are clear and never vary, and when the character in the game is "out" or runs out of time for the task: GAME OVER. The cool thing about a video game though, is that there is always another game you can play next. Even very young kids get over the loss in a video game and learn early to press "reset" or the *"Play Again?"* button to get back in the game.

Really, time-outs in life *should* be this quick. We should be able to recover from a slip up and be able to step back into another opportunity to show ourselves as winners, capable of giving it another try. Just as we reenter the highway after a humbling speeding ticket, consider that life is about being in the game as much as possible and being timed-in to this wonderful, vibrant life; this is where we want our children all the time. When a rule is broken, there's yelling or talking back, a Ghost of Parent Past would meet ire with ire. We are (usually) bigger and stronger. We can (usually) yell louder if we want, too. But if you reflect upon those encounters, you might see that they give little opportunity for children to show their capability, to learn and quickly demonstrate success. Alternatively, if we meet the sassy quip with an emotionless, energy-less withdrawal of our relationship, we give children a chance to see that they don't get in the game unless they play by the rules (inside voices, complaints versus complaining, no hitting, etc.).

"Whoops. Broke a rule. Reset."

"Hmmm. Try that again after you take a reset."

"Mom is going to go reset."

When I first began using this idea with my children, they were both full of "adolescent self-righteousness." To tell my 14-year-old daughter to reset was not really an option. But it became obvious that I could reset MYSELF in response to tone, attitude, or comment made by my daughters. I would say (or even just think to myself), "I am going to reset myself for a minute," as I walked out of the room or explained why I was hanging up the phone for a bit. Sometimes, I would make it a joint decision, "We both need to reset right now." Or, "Whoops. Try that again after we reset." It was amazing, actually, that MY ability to reset became their opportunity to get timed-in more quickly. An argument is a monologue if you turn your back and walk away from it (respectfully and being clear that you are leaving to reset). I would often not return, but wait to be sought out once she was calm. Sometimes, as hormones have the ability to steer our ships, our reset would take longer than a few minutes. But the reset built trust that the relationship was stable.

A frustrated parent scoffs, "A time-out for hitting her sister? Hitting me? Throwing something after I JUST SAID 'Don't do that'!?" Here, for many, is the biggest paradigm shift. Remember where we begin: energy for energy. What is our goal as a parent? This is "rubber meets the road." I contend our ultimate goal is to build the capacity to handle all life's challenges. This does not necessarily mean compliance to all parental requests. But again, whatever we name, we get more of, so here we don't name the broken rule with energy and relationship. We don't put ourselves (or our ego), in the way of the consequence that is ultimately removal of "us" and of life's privileges. We step up and remain firm. No relationship until the time-out ("reset, take a minute, sideline," etc.) and reparation, as you have set it up in advance, occurs.

It is worth taking a moment for a note and some perspective about physical violence and personal safety.

The Nurtured Heart Approach, by its nature, assumes that building and nurturing capacity and inner wealth will create capable kids and adults that are self-aware and self-regulating. I recognize that remaining firm and consistent with a volatile or violent child is difficult. Hitting is not okay, and especially violence that goes beyond the easy removal of relationship, requires attention. Here, in the moment, safety remains the priority over any other interventions. Remove yourself. Do not engage. If you can, ensure that your child does not have access to items that might make the situation worse. Never hesitate to call for authorities if weapons are involved. Strictness to Rules is never more strict than here. Outside of the violence, I ask you to consider that actually *no one* likes the anger, the physical response. It is a child without more tools in the toolbox. If these children knew what to do, they could self-regulate in that instance, and could consider another option. Had their pre-frontal lobes formed with consequence-risk downloaded, they would be making a better choice. They are uncomfortable in their own skin. They want something different than this moment. And they are still just a kid.

Consider your own anger outbursts. When they are done, do you feel better? Connected? Relieved? My experience tells me otherwise. And children feel even more. They are spent. Embarrassed. Guilty. Humiliated. Fearful. Very, very fearful. This lens can help us see beyond our own anger and fear. It "explains," as I often tell my challenged students, but doesn't "excuse." As a lens, however, it is mighty powerful.

Meanwhile...

In chapter two, I gave a sample of how you can introduce the idea of a "reset" to your child. I encourage you to consider coming up with your own term if you want to get greatest buy-in. Most of all, you simply need to be transparent. Let them know you are trying this out, seek their input, and be honest about the issues and goals. Then go ahead and bravely reset yourself back. Ironically reset the grocery store clerk. While you wait for the difficult child to get out of your way in the aisle, reset him "mentally." When your good friend starts to complain about another friend, tell her you gotta reset yourself. Model and be it. Accept it isn't easy, but, in your gut, you know it is the right way to head.

A Few Comments about Physical Punishment

Our world has come a far cry from "Children should be seen and not heard." Significant research has demonstrated the short-term and long-term effects of corporal punishment. While most of us were spanked as children (and many of us don't feel we were "damaged"), I find it ironic that we remember those moments of spanking with more clarity than other moments of parenting. It was humiliating. It made us angry and revengeful. We felt disrespected and terrified. And it hurt! Spanking, slapping a hand, or even flicking a head with a finger is an easy-parent-out. It often works in stopping the behavior. We, the parent, are usually bigger, stronger, and louder than our child. But I can't help but feel as if I just described the schoolyard bully. Parenting out of fear is completely different than being fearless in parenting. Parenting is our greatest job and challenge; it is hard, demanding, and exhausting. Our kids don't listen or comply and sometimes are just downright unlikeable. Is hitting them going to change that in the short term? The long term?

In reality, parenting with the Nurtured Heart Approach, or any other system, which focuses on building inner wealth in a child, is harder and takes more skill and thought than using quick physical punishment, which establishes compliance based on the fear of pain, rather than the reward of timed-in life activities. And while it may gain compliance, it does not build relationship or the confidence in a child that he can handle the rules and make the right choices. You get this, or you would not being working so hard to be a Nurtured Heart parent. So when you feel yourself rising to the easy-out of a spanking, or a warning of the same, know that that is YOUR sign to reset yourself. You need to Take A Minute, Sideline yourself, Press Pause, Give Yourself Five – whatever term you choose in your family for a reset – and in that reset remind yourself that you are giving your child the greatest gift: your intentional self-control. You are modeling how to calm down, to walk away, and regain your greatness. It isn't easy, this parenting stuff.

Strictness to Rules:
Is It <u>Ever</u> Okay to Bend Them a Little?

A parent I was coaching was having difficulty getting her child out of bed for school each day. He would hit the snooze button and ignore the repeated pleas. The intended family rule was that each child woke up at 7:15 a.m. Other children in her family (except this middle child) were able to follow this request and emerge from their rooms within five minutes of their "family rule" time. The rule had no teeth for this fourth-grade boy, Joey. He preferred to sleep more, thank you very much. Embedded in this morning battle was the additional stress of getting everyone out the door on time, and ideally, fed.

Once Joey was finally up, he always made his own cereal for breakfast (way to go on that one, mom!), but it seemed that there was no boundary on the kitchen. The kitchen was always "OPEN," and, therefore, three minutes before the departure time, the identified child would still be eating his cereal at the breakfast bar. Worse, his dawdling behavior made everyone edgy and grumpy. Other siblings were late for school, and inevitably mom would end up clearing his cereal bowl, gathering his school supplies and sports equipment, and even tying his shoes to get him where he needed to be.

His older brother would also join in both the nagging and the rescue. This system was working well for Joey, but the frazzled family was a mess.

Take any rule like this in your family and you can see how easy it is to bend it. What is the real consequence to Joey if he does not follow the rule? Angry, frustrated mom, snappy brother, full stomach, and yet still have everything retrieved for you and ready in the car? To be fearless as a parent means you are the model for holding firm to the line. It means you can handle the uncomfortable, unhappy child because you know he can handle it, too. Life is often uncomfortable, and helping our children survive and thrive builds their capacity to handle more of the same and push past it to self-responsibility. Training a child is so much about training ourselves to be relentless in building capacity, relentless in holding high expectation, and relentless in being firm to the consequence of the broken rule.

In Glasser's book *Notching Up the Nurtured Heart Approach* (c. 2011), he created a chart which reflects powerfully what it takes to stay firm: to go inward with your angst and recognize you can do this uncomfortable moment yourself so that you become the gift of strictness to your child. Not bending rules means being clear to yourself and your child that both of you can handle the consequence. It means the broken rule is not about you, nor is compliance to the rule. It remains the child to own and embrace it. It falls on you to name all the great things it says about your child when he or she follows the rule or does the hard thing. I get Joey. I hate getting up. I hit snooze, too. But my maturity and life-experience has provided me clear consequences and boundaries. For our children, we are the foundation of those steps to self-responsibility.

So armed with NHA, mom introduced the new *Sheriff of Greatness* in town, and gave the young ten-year-old two choices for making the move out of bed within five minutes of his rather loud alarm. Both choices were reasonable and both involved the same outcome; however, choice, in and of itself, is power. Choice is always a parent's best tool (when both choices provide the needed outcome or a third one which provides a energy-less consequence). "Which did he prefer?" she persisted without negative energy. Then, using her creative spirit and conviction, she flooded him with the knowledge that, not only was he was very capable of getting out of bed on his own, the kitchen was going to "CLOSE" ten minutes before it was time to leave. (I suggested she have Joey make a *Kitchen Is Closed* sign that she could put up at that set time and that all food be removed. He actually bought into that, too!)

This mom also began Glasser's "hijacking" technique in which any movement toward the good choice was noted and recognized. "Joey, I see you already moving to get up even though you want to sleep more. Your self-responsibility is right on today. You really contribute to our family goals by helping all of us be on time." And so on. Admittedly, the Sheriff of Greatness had to begin with a script. She would practice on little things that were not her main issues and was amazed at how her subtle, or sometimes less than subtle, positive recognitions empowered her child to continue to move in the right direction. So Joey agreed that he was capable of this request. This conversation did not happen during a battle zone morning, but rather in a calm afternoon.

Initially, as you might imagine, the high of the buy-in was significant because the Stands were firm and the positive flooding by all the family was consistent. Day four, Joey was tired. He stayed in bed fifteen minutes beyond his time. Mom resisted calling or checking on him. The alarm continued to sound loudly in the hallway (his choice). Mom had to be on time as she had an appointment. She went in to remind him. She told him the kitchen would be closed. Joey began to move. But at ten minutes before departure, he was not in the kitchen. At six minutes before, he raced in and grabbed a bowl. And here is where she "bent." Who wants to send a grumpy and already inattentive child to school? What does it say about us as parents when the teacher asks our child if he had breakfast, and he replies, "My mom wouldn't let me." Ah...the dilemma of appearing as a bad parent, when in reality, you are trying to be a parent who **matches choices to consequences.**

In visiting recently with some very gifted parents, who also bend the rules, one insightful mom offered this (paraphrased) piece of mercy. We are just learning to grow as parents, just as our child is growing, too. Once we know in our gut the right choice, even if it makes us uncomfortable to the scrutiny of others who don't yet know our intention, "We need to trust ourselves," she mused. We parent in isolation (thus my chapter on leading a parent group) – but we learn in community. A Fearless Parent recognizes that it is not easy to hold firm to the rules. And that clarity is really the growth piece. It is rare that a parent bending occasional rules would permanently damage a child. In fact, it is really the children's developmental job to see if they can bend the rules (curfew, bedtime, wake time, homework, swearing, running in the house, etc.). The challenge for the Fearless Parent lies in understanding their motivation, loving them for it, and accepting their discomfort as the parent works to stay consistent. Another mom in the group reminded us that, as the child's primary educator, our goal is to train them for independence.

Let's consider **a few analogies** that you can present as you set up the rules and the certain consequences to your children. Glasser's favorite illustration is that of a Nintendo game. Here in Microsoft land, we can say X-Box, too. The rules of electronic games never bend. When you run into an enemy, a specific symbol, or a cliff: You are out. Always. Every time. No exceptions. For older kids, I like to consider the rules of the road, when policed properly. Red lights are always red, and you will always get a ticket if you run the red in front of the cop. So you are the gamekeeper, the cop. Ultimately, they will play the game out of your sight and drive on streets without patrols. You are gearing them up for that. They can handle the rules because they like to play/drive. And someday they want to do it all on their own, and we want them doing it on their own, too. The greatest part of all of this is that even if the rule is broken, they get to reset and restart fresh, play another round, start the car, and get back on the road. All the hard work we do as parents is rewarded when our kids drive safely into their futures. Their future is the next moment of success, the next opportunity to demonstrate self-responsibility, and our next chance to notice exactly that. They followed the rule even though it was hard.

So let's get back to Joey's mom. The next day, she reminded Joey that his broken rule was not allowed, though her actions proved differently. She energized him with the old lecture about disappointment and family support. As you can guess, he returned to more complaining and tactical delays. When she began to volley back, she realized what she was doing in mid-retort. Here is where this Sheriff of Greatness really shone. She admitted she was wrong. She admitted to her son that she handled the situation poorly, and treated him as though he could not handle the consequence. Silly her, for thinking he was not old enough, capable enough, nor responsible enough to not only follow the family rules, but also to handle the choice when he slipped. She apologized to him. And then she got back on her "Greatness Pedestal" (as I coin our return to NHA when we have a human slip of habit). She decided to do something she had been afraid of doing before: the logical and energy-free consequence.

It took Joey several broken rules to learn that the new Sheriff was strictness, too. Joey came down when the kitchen was closed, and Joey went to school without breakfast. Joey went to school without his coat. Joey did not earn time on the computer that night or the opportunity to watch his pre-recorded show because he was not up in time to make his bed. These were the consequences, some even created by Joey himself when they set up the *New Sheriff In Town* plan.

Was this a pleasant time? Not for anyone in the family, actually. Mom had to take care not to bend just to avoid the escalated response to her strictness. She had to bite her tongue and resist defending her rules and consequences. She had to sing to the radio in the drive to her son's school to keep herself from saying, "Because I said so!" (See Chapter nine's elaboration on what to do with the "Why?" query in response to a parent request.) As Glasser says in his notch-up strategy (p.120) "...Refuse to let the child in on your angst, visually or verbally – that's private." She had to keep her energy focused on the intention - ultimate independence and self-responsibility. But the best part of this story is that it really didn't take long for Joey to get it. One day without breakfast (Mom did privately tell the teacher the intention of this consequence and was overjoyed to feel her support), three different days in a two-week period without electronics, and one particularly unpleasant day without a coat. That was it. For that rule.

The reward of maintaining consistency is that you and your rules gain respect. The rules are reasonable and so is the person enforcing them. It is not doled out by the Chief of Criticism, the Lord of Lecture, or the Dean of Disappointment. (Sorry, I couldn't help it – but the point is critical.) You are the Sheriff of Greatness, and in your town you aim to find it, name it, and live it.

A Caveat to Consider in Introducing a Credit System

Howard Glasser originally developed a credit system where points could be given for compliance to rules and points could be spent on agreed upon items (screen time, sleep overs, and other privileges of a timed-in life.) These points could only be spent if the child had served the appropriate reset or served a logical consequence to the broken rule (i.e., picked up the clothes she left lying around, cleared the table for two meals to make amends for the missed chore earlier, etc.). For many families and kids, these positive systems can be very effective, and I encourage you to explore them in greater detail in Glasser's various books. I did not feel the need to replicate this in any significant depth as he offers clear suggestions and directions.

I also want to add, as does Glasser himself, that the crux in the credit system (and why many falter after a few weeks or months) is parental follow-through. He advises to keep the "Ways to Earn Points" and the "Ways to Spend Points" few and specific. As a parent myself, and an educator, I have seen many of these fade as teachers or parents begin leaking negativity to warn about "losing points" or threaten to "freeze all spending." When and if this begins to happen, your credit system is not the problem, but rather you have forgotten to give more energy to what is going right (without the points!) so that the lens is on the real prize: self-responsibility, independence, and self-awareness.

With extreme behaviors, many well-meaning parents attempt to bribe their children into compliance with toys and extra privileges. Be clear and ready if you begin a credit system; it is about recognition. Keep the prizes reasonable and grounded realities of a real timed-in world. Avoid points that turn into money to buy things – and consider the option of life's privileges as pretty darn worth a real buy-in. Rides to friends' houses, pick-up later from school, a treat after practice, a chance to see a new movie, an extended curfew, an extra 20 minutes on a game, more phone time, a trip to the library or park, folded laundry, and a choice of beverage at a meal: these are valuable commodities in a life well lived, and ones worth earning as a member of "team" family.

Parenting WITH Technology: Keeping Up with Rules That "Trend"

Parenting is different today. For those of us lucky to have grandparents into our adulthood, and then perhaps, great-grandparents to our children, we have noted their comments of disapproval directed towards the resources that distract and engage our children. These are new and unfamiliar to even our time as children: the overscheduling of sports and activities, the early access to electronic games, and the handheld devices that distract from a more personal connection. The impact of our children's vastly different use of free time has yet to be fully revealed as the first youth of this electronic generation are just exiting college. Something in our gut recognizes that this steady shift away from face to face interaction will likely impact the developmental pace of early skills needed to develop empathy, read body language and facial expressions, manage emotions, handle transitions, and also self-regulate during "boring" times. While this is not intended to be an essay rallying against the tools of technology (which I, too, depend upon), I think we cannot ignore its impact to our parenting challenges.

Quick show of hands: Does your five-year-old own a handheld game? Does your family have a game box or console with your television? Do your children spend time on the computer playing games? Do they know how to turn on the computer? Do they know how to play games on your phone? Would they choose these options as playtime over having a friend come over and play imaginary games in the backyard? If any of these are true, then you know parenting is different today. Figuring out how to mesh the ever more tantalizing toy, the fast-paced activities, and the constant want of "more" and "new" and "I am bored" can frustrate a parent who just wants to read with their children. There is also the issue of how much knowledge is too much knowledge. What is age-appropriate? How can I set boundaries if his best friend's parents let them play games that he is not developmentally ready for? How can I help him to grow up slowly and appreciate each stage of discovery? And why does he have to challenge my every attempt to set these boundaries?

If you reread the last four questions, you may actually hear the voice of your own parent generations ago. Nothing will stand still developmentally or culturally. But some things, like parents lamenting the exposure of inappropriate things to their children, remain a constant parent woe. Armed with the knowledge that we are more alike than different, it is helpful to see technology as an ally rather than an enemy. As the saying goes, "Keep your friends close and your enemies CLOSER!"

Get clear on your boundaries as soon as you can, I would like to say, "from the start", but likely the wiggle room is bigger than you intended. Make it a family plan. There will always be another toy. There will always be more and new and better. As I write this, I think in hindsight about some of the technology tools I purchased because of the "shiny, new" appeal, and the neighbors' boastful celebration of their own technology, compelled me. The research on screen time and children is just beginning to surface. Excessive amounts of television viewing has been linked to obesity. Exposure to violent shows has been associated with greater incidents of violence as well as repetition of actions and words, many which are not age-appropriate for younger audiences.[8] However, the impact of violent gaming appears to be substantially more negative than passively watching violent television shows. The lure of the video game is undeniable, particularly for boys who are more drawn, and more easily addicted, to the spatially visual media and competition. It is easy to find recent research in magazines[9], online, and

---

[8] I expand on this topic in my admittedly biased editorial, *The Output Often Mirrors the Input* in Chapter 10 of this book.

[9] Anderson, C. A., Shibuya, A., Ihori, N., Swing, E. L., Bushman, B. J., Sakamoto, A., Rothstein, H. R., Saleem, M., & Barlett, C. P. (2010). Violent video game effects on aggression, empathy, and prosocial behavior in Eastern and

through university-published resources that have studied the impact of violent video games on child behavior. Many of us don't need the citations to experience the reality. It makes sense. In the same way we are saying that we get more of what we name, we get more of what we do, too. "...violent games directly reward violent behavior, such as by awarding points or by allowing players to advance to the next game level. In some games, players are rewarded through verbal praise, such as hearing the words "Nice shot!" after killing an enemy."[10] Not exactly our intent when we nurture good choices, right?

Additionally, the powerful communication tools of social networking (phone, text, instant message, Facebook, Twitter, blogs, etc.) intrigue and capture the verbal talents and draw of girls in particular. While the above examples of violent video gaming tap into the hard wiring of most boys, the social network side of technology is one of bonding and connection: This is a clear area of need fulfillment in most females. [11]

All of this noted, it remains an issue of boundaries. Many of us have experienced the impact of removing something completely from a child's world in the effort to gain power

---

Western countries: A meta-analytic review. *Psychological Bulletin, 136*(2), 151-173

[10] Anderson, C. A., & Bushman, B. J. (2002). Media violence and societal violence. Science, 295, 2377-2378

[11] Psychologist and brain gender researcher, Michael Gurian is referenced in more detail in Chapter 7 in regards to impact in school settings.

and compliance. Sometimes this works – sometimes they don't "bite." In the reality of technology, we want them to use it, learn from it, be challenged by it. Our ultimate goal is to shape a child's ability to make good choices around the use of technology: to balance and manage time, to moderate use and to see it as a bonus, not as a lifestyle. This is not a simple goal. Erring on the side of bias and tempered rationally by experience, I believe this needs to be a hard line you draw. When you negotiate choices, consider that when it comes to time management and the lure of technology, kids are in over their heads most of the time. They have not yet learned to balance. (Remember yourself on Halloween? "Get candy, get candy, get candy," as Jerry Seinfeld's humorous monologue reminds.) Today's technology tools, machines with lights and noises and things they can control, are the best candy of their generation. It doesn't matter if you take the candy away, other parents have candy at their homes; candy stores are out there, all their friends are willing to share their candy, too. We are just trying to ensure that theirs is not a diet of only candy!

Computer and cyber technology is one of the fastest growing fields in our world. As I type this, using my much-loved and outdated computer, I know that something is being invented right now that we cannot even imagine. The impact of technology on how people relate has been huge. Immediate contact, tweeting locations, uploading a photo, searching private information; it is all right there for us, and for our kids. When we think back over the past 20 years, we can be amazed at the world's rapid dependence on computers, cell phones, and the Internet. Most of today's children have never seen a rotary dial phone or televisions with knobs on them to change a channel: "What? You had to get up all the time?" Most will never want for the immediate ability to reach a parent who travels with a cell phone, and the majority of this generation will own a cell phone by the time they are in sixth grade.

On top of all of this, they will be incredibly savvy with these complicated tools, but also feel dependent on their access. When my daughter is traveling or I need to reach her about walking the dog, I can text her. If she gets a flat tire or someone rear-ends her, she can call me right there on the scene. It is both a peace of mind and a burden. It adds significant bulk to the list of parental boundaries needed as technology tools and trends change rapidly. We can't dummy down here. We need to keep pace as we raise our children, ideally, pushing to lead the race in current tricks (i.e., checking search history, knowing all the passwords and adding parental protections, etc.[12]) Finally, we need to model the boundaries ourselves. We need to be fully present during our family time, when we drive, during meals, and in our conversations. (Personal pet peeve: talking on our cell phones when someone is helping us. I know this is common; however, I am not sure what we are modeling except entitlement if we are not gracious in public.) If we want our kids present in relationship, then we have to put the shiny

---

[12] The Anti-Drug website is a great resource for more specific parenting suggestions: www.theantidrug.com/advice/teens-today/teens-and-technology/parent-tips.aspx

toy aside. If necessary, make it a family rule for everyone. Use timers and rewards. Although it is hard to compete, when we reduce a child's screen/tech time, our relationship becomes more tangible and rewarding for everyone.

So what is a reasonable amount of time? This can be part of your family plan; deciding on daily or weekly minutes, being clear how they are earned. Until a child's work requires access to a computer to complete assignments, computers (and phones and games) should remain a rich privilege of a timed-in life. They are earned, enjoyed, and valued for their entertainment. Just as candy is a luxury and a treat, neither is necessary for survival. "I need a laptop," my high-school-aged daughter literally just said to me a couple of hours ago. "Naw," I think. "Hmm..," I say noncommittally and redirect the conversation, as we have had this debate before. "Not yet," I think. We have a couple at home she can always use; she doesn't go without. Right now, she needs to continue to show us she knows how to earn one. We already battle her cell phone. Anyway, by the time she graduates, the technology is going to blow her socks off. She can wait. And we can honor her patience and resourcefulness until that day arrives.

Supporting and Empowering Your Child in School-Related Issues

As an educator AND parent, I often rode the fence frequently to balance my role as Tiger Mom and Emancipating Teacher. Having been the brunt of parental accusations in the past, I worked hard at living my truth: seeing everyone as well intentioned (and sometimes just not as skilled.) The thing about riding fences, however, is you can get splinters in your butt ☺. (I would often use this analogy when I had students use rating scales that had no mid-point.) Sometimes you have to take a stand and pick the side to work from. In our book for educators, *There's Always Something Going Right* (Triandis and Small, c. 2010), we wore the hat of the teacher working with the sometimes-challenging parent. Here, I hope to offer some strategies and viewpoints that will help you partner with your children's teachers, communicate strongly and most importantly model self-advocacy for your children in such a way that they garnish critical communication skills and greater responsibility in their own learning goals.

"How Was School Today, Sweetheart?"

We would be rich as kings if we were rewarded for every vague "Fine" which comes in response to this question. We probe and query, curious to know what our children have been occupied with in the past six or seven hours. We get very little. To step up the newsworthy details many years ago, I borrowed an idea from a movie I had seen where the family played "highs and lows." Each member of the family would share two things that went well (the "highs") and one thing that wasn't so hot (the "lows"). It was a fun way to glean more about our days, but as I became a clearer Nurtured Heart practitioner, I began to realize that giving <u>any</u> energy to the complaining of the past rarely benefited any of us. I am not implying that our world as Nurtured Heart families is made of only happy times, merely that requiring us to focus or rehash the bad moment of our day didn't serve the intention of tapping into what was going well. We modified our game, then, to simply required two "highs." Low points were allowed but not required or coaxed; in fact, it became more fun to see who could come up with more great things that happened to them that day.

While the "Best Day Competition" can be fun, there are genuine times when exploring solutions for problems is needed. Note the framing: Solutions versus Complaining. Problem-solving versus venting. Problems are real and relationships have challenges. Your child is feeling targeted by a teacher; she is being left out by a group of friends; some kids are picking on another one of her classmates. These are real problems ("lows") that deserve a compassionate response. But use caution. Under the good intention of showing compassion and empathy, we often end up energizing the problem with lots of relationship ourselves. The child, unwittingly, learns that he gets a whole lot more of our attention when he is complaining about an unfair grading situation or mean-kid story, than he gets when he share a non-conflict story about a successful book report. We want life to be easy for them, and we are not there in the schoolhouse to ensure that everyone is "nice" and "fair" and "inclusive." The Mama or Papa Bear in us is often justifiably awakened to great energy around the stories our children bring home that involve mistreatment. While we should not be dismissive about their feelings, we serve our children best when we remain calm, neutral, and empowering. This is their problem to own and solve, and when we swoop in to tell them what to do, or get on the phone with the parent of the bully, or call the teacher to complain, we send a subliminal message to our child: "You can't handle this."

I recently coached a Mama Bear "off the attack" so to speak, when she came in one morning after dropping her fourth grader off at her class. Visibly upset, she shared incident after incident where her daughter had been the target of a particular "mean girl" in that grade. The girl got other girls to gang up on her daughter, leave her out, and send mean messages her way. Her child didn't want to go to school any longer. These stories always break my heart a bit because I know that this child has suffered a long time. She has tried to handle it on her own. She likely waited until it felt unbearable to tell an adult. This mom, however, revealed something that I find to be happening frequently: Each day that she picks up her child (let's call her Emma), she asks her how "Erin" (the identified mean girl) treated her today. She probes for the problem. Her intention of empathy and support was clear, but the child has ironically been coached to look for failure versus success. When the mom drops off Emma each morning, she has gotten into the habit of "scaffolding" her up, telling her she can handle Erin. "Ignore her, find other friends, play another game, stay in at recess, etc." These are great tips, truly, and ones I often explore with students myself. These are solutions, right? This is problem solving, right? Isn't this what I was saying we should do? Yes – and no. This is mom, assuming problems. This is mom, focusing on the problem and building relationship around the problem. Do I blame mom? Heavens, no. She is well intentioned. She is trying to help. She did not recognize that by placing the lens on the problem, she was actually increasing relationship and energy in that direction, too.

Here is where I use the approach on mom: "You are an amazing parent, so concerned and compassionate about your child's struggle. It must frustrate you because you can't keep her safe from this. Seeking support from the adults who are HERE in our building is such a great idea, as we can give her the opportunity to have a positive resolution right where the issue is happening. Before we trouble-shoot, tell me more about Emma." Here I want to distract mom from her focus on deficit thinking. Anytime she begins to go down the path of complaining, rehashing past complaints, or telling the story, I redirect her to her child's strengths and gifts. This subtle shift is how real change occurs. See your child as capable. "Has she ever had a friendship issue in the past that she was able to move past?" Don't look for details or back-story; focus on how she handled it. Remember: whatever you name, you get/see more off. I help this mom to see capacity, resilience, creativity, persistence, and her child's ability to confront problems with solutions. Generally, after I coach mom around NHA she can begin to recognize the need to take the situation in another direction. Does the problem happen at home? Nope. Who is having the problem? The child. Who needs to feel good about solving the problem the most? The child. Who needs to step away and remind the child she has all she needs to solve this problem? The mom. Who can help the child connect to significant adults who are actually IN the schoolhouse? The mom.

Another direction might look like this: Emma comes to the parent, upset that Kate has told her other friends to not play with her anymore. Empathize with Emma's feelings (real loss and isolation). Try not to offer more than that. Distract and move to something that went well. If Emma is too hyper-focused on this, share something that went well for you. After she is calm and off the topic, you can return to it from a calm, solution-focused approach: "That sounds so frustrating, this situation with Kate. I am so impressed with how you are handling it, Emma. You could hide from it or not talk about finding a solution, but you are ready to solve it. What do you think you should do?"

I remember a wise counselor saying to me once many years back, "Most people know exactly what they need to do." She implied that while they believed they were coming in for advice, what they often sought was simply assurance and confidence. In all my years of counseling kids and families, I find this to be a frequent and stable mindset. When we are under stress, we don't think as clearly. Often a child, hot off the playground from a child who cheated or was a bad sport, will come storming into my office, leave a long note on my desk, or race to a playground supervisor. "Hear my side of the story." "This is not fair." "He cheated." Ironically, this simple act of leaving the game has actually been a problem-solving step. If they do manage to catch me in his/her high-emotional state, I tell them this exactly: "John, that sounds so unfair. And look what you did. You knew exactly what you needed to do: leave the situation and come and calm down. You impress me with your maturity. You could have made this worse, but instead you are talking it out. What do you think you should do next recess?" Kids are brilliant when they are calm. "Play with someone else. Go join the other kids playing soccer. Tell Jimmy I am not going to play with him because I don't think he plays fairly. Finish my science project with my team." And so on.

Certainly, I can provide a broad list of solutions. I am a neutral party who believes in the capacity of ALL my students to follow the rules of fair and compassionate play. I also know that I am just hearing one side of the story. As with Emma and Kate, Kate will have her own story to tell, a past hurt or feeling left out herself. Keeping in mind that we all want to belong and connect, and that some are just not as skilled is key in having empathy for both sides of a situation and working toward solutions.

I can recall an angry parent coming to see me about a bullying issue. In his best Papa Bear mode, the father had wanted the school to discipline the bully severely, perhaps even expel him. I explained that I would first need to meet with his son and learn more about his feelings (not just depend on the parent version) and then also speak with this identified bully and learn his side of the story. "What? You think there is more than one truth??!" the father retorted. Hmmm... well, yes. I retell this story often as a reminder that everyone has a truth and none are exactly the same. Our children bring home their version of the truth. We must honor that. And we must remember, there is always more to every story.

Regarding bullying: I do not intend to sound dismissive to real concerns about bullying. Bullying is NOT okay. It is <u>repeated</u> behavior designed to intentionally hurt a person, generally to gain power. Many states now require a specific anti-bullying policy and required curriculum. Media have hit bullying with stories in the news and documentaries at the movie theater. National and local conferences target this topic regularly, and they are well attended. President Obama speaks about it in speeches. Dozens of books are published each year on this topic. (In fact, as a therapeutic project to support a target of such behavior in one of our third grade classes, I led the students through the creation and illustration of such a book. My principal supported the publication of *Give Your Hearts Out to Everyone: Third*

Graders' Rules to Making the Right Choices at School (c. 2012) as a powerful teaching tool for other groups of younger kids learning to navigate the challenging world of peer relationships in school.) Psychologists have studied incarcerated juveniles and adults and correlate a direct relationship between children who were identified as bullies in elementary school and those serving prison sentences. There are real bullying behaviors and real fear and devastation on targets. Ironically, the majority of the kids I work with are mortified to find out that another student or students consider them bullies. The parents are even more surprised. No one wants to be a bully and no one really feels safe around him or her either.

When I coach kids who are targets of bullying, I focus on the capacity of that child to step away from the message and behavior of the bully. I teach them all kinds of ways to respond and react. I remind them that every person is 100 percent responsible for every word out of his/her mouth, and every action. The responsibility for a bullying act falls to the bully. It is not about the target. It is the bully who is choosing this behavior. The target can choose their response, similarly. "Are you stupid?" I may query a kid who was called that in class. "No," they mumble. I ask them to say that louder and like they really mean it. Very powerful. If they can recognize that they are not "stupid, fat, clumsy, dumb, weird, etc.," and I can, with their help, provide irrefutable evidence of them NOT being whatever the mean kid was calling them, then they don't have to own that trait. "I am not stupid." Well, of course not. A stupid person would never have thought to come and get support from an adult! "Did you make _____ (the bully) say this to you?" "No." "So is it your fault?" "No!" And so on. Additionally, I like to make kids smile a bit when I point out that this bully seems to pay a lot of attention to him/her. "She must really like you or something, huh? All that focus on you!" They usually giggle at this and it reduces the bully's power over the target if the target can see this person in a different light.

Kids pick on kids often because they are different. Different makes people feel uncomfortable and part of the goal of the social curriculum in school is to help people embrace differences, honor differences, accept differences, and even celebrate differences. We can't make people be nice, but we can decide what we take in and what messages we will surround ourselves with. Maybe our job is to bully our kids into recognizing their own greatness. That is a form of the word I can own!

When All Else Fails, Build Relationship: Partner with Your Child's School

It is always helpful to remember the powerful lens of naming what is going right whenever you are frustrated or challenged by a reported situation with one of your son's or daughter's teachers/administrators. A classroom teacher can have as many as 180 students for whom he/she is responsible; an administrator and school counselor can have caseloads upwards of 500. Maintaining this perspective is helpful when you approach a teacher about YOUR one child, accepting that it is not the teacher's intention to single out your child, fail your child, embarrass your child, or make assumptions about your child. Assuming this good intention, it can be very powerful to establish relationship right at the beginning of the year whenever possible. I suggest to the parents of the families I coach that perhaps they make an early appointment. Bring in a Starbucks gift card (hey, I am from Seattle) and a copy of any of the Nurtured Heart books for educators. (I am a fan of mine, but all are very well written.)

You can let him/her know that this is a system of relationship that you are using in your family to bring out the best version of everyone you are in relationship with, and thought he/she would love the concepts and tools, as it is good for all children. You can honor her by acknowledging that she likely has a system or philosophy that she utilizes, but speaking from the point of view of an educator myself, we are the epitome of lifelong learners, and new approaches and ideas are usually welcomed as thoughtful. She may have heard of the Nurtured Heart Approach before, even, and having a short statement of its three Stands can make it simple. "It really is just an approach which is helping us give energy to what we see going well, and not warn or nag or get angry for broken rules, but keep our expectations high and our consequences consistent." Bring your child, if you can, to simply introduce them, and using the "hijack'" method (a Glasser term described in earlier chapter), share some genuine positive examples to set up the relationship for success. (*Remember: Whatever you name you get more of!*)

"Good afternoon, Mr. Johnson. Thanks for taking a few minutes in your day to meet us. Your quick response to my request with all you have going on was impressive. I find everyone in this school to be so wonderful with communication. Kenny is always a bit nervous when he starts a new year, so I really appreciate that you are welcoming and flexible, too."

And so on, in your own voice, of course. Simply establishing a relationship, which is not based on a problem, sets you up as a partner with the professional teacher. Sharing privately with the teacher later, in an email or phone call, any specific strategies or knowledge that will help the teacher to be more successful with your son or daughter is great, too. Accommodations or special needs are critical for a teacher to know in advance so that he or she can start on the right foot. Here are some examples of classroom supports that parents have suggested: Sticking to rules, consistency, repeated directions, needing to move, not being allowed to roam, reading silently as a way to calm down, sitting in proximity, using cues or special signals, cards on the desk with steps, rewarding with relationship, ignoring behaviors that disrupt, working in a private space, sitting near the board, not giving warnings, leadership opportunities, and so on.

Then, when and if a situation arises where you need to address an academic, social, or behavioral issue with the teacher, you are working in tandem as problem solvers. There is no blame or accusation. Deep experience has taught me that no one takes in criticism in a way that builds relationship. Remember, as the primary educator and advocate of your child, it falls on you each year to meet with your child's teacher to keep successful accommodations in place. Unless your child is on a specific I.E.P. (Individualized Education Plan based on special education qualification and an identified learning disability or health impairment), much of "what worked" last year with a teacher is not carried to the next without parental nudging. Even a parent with a child receiving accommodations under the A.D.A.s 504 Plan (Americans with Disabilities Act – Section 504, which allows for accommodations in schools and workplaces based on health impairments) should plan to advocate for which accommodations are most beneficial. Additionally, every teacher is different in style and personality; as in life, every person we work with requires taking some time to learn and know. This diversity provides our child early opportunities to learn to be flexible, patient, tolerant, and persistent.

As parents, we rarely get to choose our kid's teachers. (They didn't choose your kid either.) If you have been a part of your school community for a while, you can hear stories that may favor one teacher over the next. Here is where it is critical that you stay on that Greatness Pedestal yourself, one that I coach kids on when they choose to stay away from gossip or rumors. Remember the caveat about each person's individual truth. Yours will be different. Avoid talking negatively about your son's or daughter's teacher in front of them. Actually don't talk AT ALL, because it skews the lens and doesn't support the necessary bridge you need to create to sustain a strong relationship with the teacher. You can have a complaint (n.) = a problem you want solved. Be out of the habit, whenever possible, of complaining (v.) = simply negative energy which builds on problems and pulls us emotionally into a loop.

As you take some time to consider the stories your children bring home about their day at school, model the shift for them from complaining to problem. Help them see problems as opportunities to learn and build relationship. Talk positively about their teacher and other kids that are demonstrating good choices. Create a habit of naming what is going right, before you hop on the Whine Wagon. Build capacity to handle life's inevitable struggles with relationships and time management and organization and different demands of different personalities. Focus on feelings, so that these are always validated, versus opinions, which can be illogical. Feeling left out? Frustrated? Picked on? Embarrassed? Yes. Teacher hates me! Everyone is laughing at me! I am in the dumb reading group! No. Help your child, who absorbs your every word (see article in Chapter 10: *Things That Make You Go Hmmmm...*), see you step away from joining in the gossip, complaining, or sharing judgment. Stay neutral if unable to stay positive, as these overheard or direct comments can often taint a child's own view of his or her power and attitude.

As I reflect on some of the strategies I employ in working with parents and students around school-related issues, I want to broaden our perspective and share some of the work of other researchers and clinicians who can help support your knowledge and skills in communicating with your sons and daughters. I find the knowledge I have gathered from the thorough work of these clinical leaders (Michelle Garcia Winner, creator of *Social Thinking* tools and Michael Gurian, pioneer of gender-based differences and solutions) merges well with my work as a Nurtured Heart trainer and coach. Having attended workshops by both, read many of their books, and incorporated their main constructs in how I both see and work with kids and adults, I will share a few key concepts that I hope will help you better understand your child as a student and peer and encourage you to go deeper.

Michelle Garcia Winner's *Social Thinking*™

When a stranger asks, "How are you?" as a greeting in a store, an automated response of "Fine," usually follows. Somewhere in our "training" we gained this social skill. A smile is usually replied with the like, a wave, the same, and in those instances, we feel good about that person, and also, pretty good about ourselves. Similarly, when a person interrupts rudely and repeatedly or a person cuts in line in a store, we have uncomfortable thoughts about that person. We tend to shy away from them, and create a relationship distance. Simple stuff, yes, but for our children just learning to navigate the world of friendships and authority figures outside of their parents, this kind of innate social cognition can be a challenge. "Social Thinking" is the user-friendly term for social cognition. A system of teaching these concepts of social thinking and social-related skills was pioneered by Michelle Garcia Winner in the 1990s (www.socialthinking.com). While her strong, sustainable work was designed initially for working with kids with

Attention Deficit Disorder and those on the Autism spectrum, I find the framework helpful in coaching all children toward greater self-awareness in relationship. Based on some commonly held beliefs and proven behaviors, *Social Thinking* provides a tool that we can use to coach our kids toward greatness and positive choices. It teaches kids, and communication-challenged adults, how to act by increasing their other-aware understanding. While most children by third grade become fluent in many of these nuances of socialization, some with deficits in communication require direct instruction.

With permission, and from her website, I list here a few of the core concepts which clarify how powerful the understanding of how we operate as social beings plays in the relationships of our children, both in and out of school.

Core facts and philosophies of social thinking:

1. Social thinking develops from birth, much like walking; it is intuitively "hard wired" into most people to work at learning how the social world works.

2. Being able to play effectively with peers in preschool provides children with a skill base necessary to sit and learn in a classroom.

3. Students with developmental delays in social thinking do not intuitively learn social information the way neurotypical children do. Instead, they have to be cognitively taught how to think socially and understand the use of related social skills.

Here are some of the core constructs that all children must fully understand (or be taught) to successfully navigate this world with others. (Note: <u>Direct quotes are in italics. This author's comments are added with underlined notations.</u>)

a) *We "think with our eyes" to figure out other people's thoughts, intentions, emotions, plans, etc.*

b) *Our thoughts and emotions are strongly connected. How we think affects how we feel, how we behave affects how others think and feel.*

   <u>A great coaching reminder</u>: *If your friends are people who make you feel good about you over time,* then you must learn how to make *friends and how to make other people feel good using your actions and your language.*

   <u>Alternatively, if you want your teachers/peers/family to feel good about you in general, your actions and language actually tell them how to feel.</u>

c) *We think about people all the time, even when we have no plans to interact with them. We adjust our own behavior based on what we think the people around us are thinking.*

   <u>See yourself in the grocery line, waiting at a four-way stop with other cars, or even walking your dog.</u>

d) *As part of our humanity, each of us is on a daily quest to avoid each other's "weird thoughts." We constantly consider people around us and adjust our behavior to help people have "normal thoughts about us."* Note: when I teach this to kids, I use Winner's other term: *uncomfortable thoughts.*

e) *Most of the core social thinking lessons operate BELOW the level of cultures, meaning that all people engage in these thoughts and social behavioral adjustments.*

f) *How we adapt our behavior changes as we age and are in different situations and cultures. The nuance and sophistication of our behaviors, which we refine greatly by 3rd grade and then across our entire lives, is constantly evolving.*

g) *Social thinking is something all of us do every day, all day, even when we are alone in our homes. To understand a TV drama or sitcom one has to think about the character's emotions, thoughts, reactions, etc. Even reading novels requires social thinking.*

I find these concepts to be so valuable in working with children within the social curriculum, and highly encourage you to dig deeper into Michelle Garcia Winner's body of work. I have chosen to share the *Social Thinking* constructs in tandem with the Nurtured Heart Approach as it honors the capability of the child to learn; it focuses on their successful relationship experiences and builds a bridge toward his/her certain future of navigating all the challenges of relationships with some clear tools. Life has rules. The rules are clear. You are rewarded for following the rules. The reward is almost always more relationship. BAM!

Michael Gurian's: Brain-based Gender Wiring

Given the understanding of Garcia Winner's work on how we interact and connect as human beings, I want to scaffold that information further with the work and insight of Michael Gurian and his analysis and application of nature-based brain differences in boys and girls.

Let me begin with a story.

My eighth grade student had broken a school rule for the third time in a week. I can recall so vividly his head sinking onto the table, frustrated at his own lack of self-control. He wasn't defiant; he didn't try to deny the reality. He was just so darn mad at himself! "Why do I keep messing up?" he asked me rather rhetorically. My heart went out to him. As Winner might have noted, he did some "unexpected" behaviors and people had some "uncomfortable thoughts"; and as Howard Glasser would have noted, in the youth's intense need for relationship, he didn't yet possess the inner wealth to chose positivity over negativity in his drive for the connection. Perhaps, the short answer is because he was a pubescent boy who was impulsive and whose frontal cerebral cortex was not yet fully established. But as I have begun to learn with Michael Gurian's meta-study, the long answer is much more interesting.

Michael Gurian (www.gurianinstitute.com) is a renowned clinical psychologist and author of 25 books, most of which focus on gender differences. His presentation, *The Minds of Boys and Girls,* draws from significant brain research, not just behavioral observations, which reflect the genetic differences in the actual structure of boys' brains versus girls' brains. For myself as an educator working with both genders for the past 28+ years (not to mention my spouse), I have a myriad of theories and observations regarding core differences. However, having actual science support my experience is confirmation tenfold.

This is not gender stereotyping (a flashback to our '70s' push), but rather some significant information that can help us understand our boys and girls better. Statistics bear out a reality familiar to us: Boys are less successful in traditional school models, are diagnosed more often with learning disabilities and A.D.H.D., are suspended more frequently, and earn fewer college degrees. Girls are diagnosed more significantly with high anxiety and eating disorders. The trend toward "mean girls" reflects a foreign concept to most boys, in that girls are silent, vicious, and excluding when they bully. They turn quickly on other girls and are territorial toward friendships. They also forgive less easily and hold grudges more frequently. These are generalities for certain, but Gurian's research upholds that these strong common gender responses/behaviors occur in about 80 percent of each gender. There are, of course, boys and girls, approximately 20 percent, who do not follow these generalized behaviors. Keeping that in mind, however, here is what brain researchers are finding out, as well as a few ideas of what it means to us as we relate to our children (and the opposite sex!).

Structurally, girls have both verbal and sensory connections throughout both sides of their brains, making them more able to make rapid connections between words, ideas, and other sensory input. This heavy verbal quality increases worry and anxiety and hyper-focus on how they look/connect.

- The default male brain has little or no verbal connections on the right side, with great activity in the cerebellum (a doing center) more gray matter, which does not process sensory or emotive. It has more motivation and habitual risk and less rumination activity (worry). Because of this hardwiring, most boys (the 80 percent noted earlier) are less attuned to others reactions if the reactions are subtle. Boys often don't read facial expressions as well, nor recognize emotions as clearly. Boys, even more certainly than most girls, learn by doing rather than observing.

- Testosterone levels in boys are 10-20 times greater than in girls. Testosterone is an aggression hormone. For girls, their dominant chemical is a bonding hormone called Oxytocin. During high levels of external or internal stress, both sexes are flooded with their respective chemical. Girls, again using the 80 percent majority concept, internalize feelings and thoughts and work to connect face to face when wanting resolution. Conversely, boys' initial response is to externalize and move to a more fight/flight response.

- Gurian notes that boys do seek to bond relationally, however this is done more often through aggression-nurturing activities (doing physical/mechanical things side by side), while girls bond by talking or interacting face to face.

- Males are much more touch-oriented to gain sensory input, and connection, so they push more, bump, tease, and banter. This seems like negative aggression to the female mind. But most of the time, 80 percent to 20 percent, it is mutual and indicative of connection for boys.

- Attention span, because of the cross-brain connection in girls, is three to four times greater in women. In fact, in SPECT scans of both genders, the resting brain shows significantly more activity in the brain of a girl sitting still, than that of a boy also resting. Boys' brains tend to move to a resting stage after five minutes of engagement on a single topic, while the brains of girls show continual signs of activation across both sides. Schools are designed for this female brain.

- Boys need to have things be louder and faster than girls, who prefer dialogue. Consider the movies, games, and activities that most males are drawn to.

- One thing however, that both-gender brains have in common: They are wired for music from the start.

Gurian, working closely with doctors in the field of brain research and behavior, connects the dots for many educators, parents, and children themselves. A growing body of schools across the country have adopted these approaches, empowering kids to better understand what they need to do when the environment doesn't match how they take in information. I believe if you dig deeper yourself, you can expect some *Aha!* insight. I would also encourage you to be open to the one powerful *Aha!* that could possibly transform how you look at behaviors: *Perhaps we need to stop blaming boys for being boys and girls for being girls; maybe we need to start meeting them right where they are.*

One More Worthy Match: Kids At Hope™ (Versus "At Risk")

I want to add another worthwhile foundation that couples well with the Nurtured Heart Approach: *Kids At Hope.* (www.kidsathope.org)

Kids at Hope (KAH) was founded by Rick Miller, from Arizona State University, under a sincere belief that we were going about our work with youth all wrong. (Okay, that is my translation of Miller's more elegant direction.) Programs are created based on deficits versus abundance. At its core, *Kids At Hope* wants every youth program to support the core construct that all children are capable of success: NO EXCEPTIONS! KAH also recognizes the power of significant adults in transforming how kids feel about this future destination (and my NHA caveat, *current* location). Wally Endicott, the Northwest Executive Director of KAH, stumbled upon my work as a Nurtured Heart Trainer, with the same insight: How teachers connect with kids is important, and every adult in our child's world has the potential to postively impact the way a child views his or herself and future. We want kids at hope <u>always</u> – not kids at risk.

"Kids at Hope's vision is that every child is afforded the belief, guidance and encouragement that creates a sense of hope and optimism, supported by a course of action needed to experience success at life's four major destinations: Home & Family; Education & Career; Community & Service; and Hobbies & Recreation...Schools, communities and programs which work with KAH uphold critical value statements which click for parents....

- *Every child is **at hope**, no exceptions.*

- *Hope depends on every adult's contribution.*

- *Respect, support and enhance relationships with all organizations that serve children.*

- *Demonstrate passion in all that we do.*

- *Ensure all practices are well researched, evidence based and outcome driven."*

Using some exciting, but also alarming on-going research from the Gallup poll on Hope, KAH is working to shift our thinking away from deficit to abundance; its intention is to bring whole communities around to helping kids live and see life as full of hope. (See document in the appendices which aligns the structural framework of *Kids At Hope* with the core relationship system of *The Nurtured Heart Approach*.)

Schoolwork: Who Owns the Problem?

A repeated body of research highlights the underdeveloped executive functioning area of the brain (the portion of our brain that aids in organization, time management, and future-thinking) as the cause for many of our children's schoolwork issues. Whatever is at the core, the battle is one that frequently frustrates both parent and student. There are innumerable books published to coach parents and students through academic struggles, whether organic in nature or attitudinal, and the best offer timeless advice matching the still-present developmental goal of independence and responsibility. When working with both parents and students around this issue, I remind both of them that, "Your mom and dad have already done fourth grade. This time it's yours to shine." Additionally, many cultures place a significant level of family honor on a child's success (or lack of) in school. "He must get 4's or he will not get into a good high school," well-meaning parents say in despair. "We have her in math tutoring three days after school and in language school each weekend." "We do not want you to think we are bad parents who do not care about our child's future."

Finding the balance that motivates student responsibility versus parental control is, perhaps, the greatest challenge we have in setting boundaries. I work to help well-intentioned parents recognize the good choices their son or daughter is making right now. What has gone well today or yesterday? Making a shift from projecting far into the future requires staying present and keeping the focus on getting more of what we are already doing right. This paradigm shift is challenging to many, but if you work at helping your child name success and feel good about it, you will get more of this success. The negative energy around school will shift, too, as you celebrate the hard work they have pushed through already. Then, as they begin to trust you see their intention and effort, you help them goal-set and organize for the remaining work ahead. Lying about completed work will diminish because your child is rewarded for telling the truth. Even if the child didn't do the assignment, his/her honesty allows for a positive outcome in the long run. Often parents think they are "goal-setting" as they outline a child's plan for success. Our ultimate goal is to create an independent thinker and learner, one who knows what needs to be done and how to tackle it. If we set up the plan and we consequence the plan and we structure the plan, whose plan is it?

In my book, *There's Always Something Going Right: Workbook For Implementing the Nurtured Heart Approach in School Settings* (co-authored with Louisa Triandis, another Advanced Nurtured Heart Trainer and school social worker), we tackle this problem by using a model for a

Student Success Meeting, where all come together to name the strengths of the student, identify goals for the student, and use the existing strengths to help the student name and achieve those goals. The students are full participants, meaning they also name their own strengths and goals. The point of this meeting, and one you could do similarly in your own family, is ownership of the plan. It is not a parent plan or a teacher plan; it is a student plan.

A few suggestions from my years in these trenches:

- Pulling from the Kids At Hope model, which helps kids learn to Time Travel (i.e., see a certain and reachable future), I think connecting hope to your childrens' future is critical. "What do you want to be when you get older?" still remains a powerful future-oriented thought. What jobs intrigue them? Where do they get lost and absorbed into something? When they play "imagine," what <u>do</u> they imagine? Keeping a future (beyond the inevitable <u>more</u> school) in the front of their minds can be a simple, positive way to make a connection.

- I find time management skills to be the number one struggle for most kids, as well as many adults. Technology can be a resource to support our management of time, but we also know that it can just as easily suck a few hours away. (Ever have anyone send you a funny video from YouTube™ and find yourself drawn into several more related and compelling clips, before some timekeeper in your mind says, "What just happened?") I believe most children don't yet have that internal timekeeper. Making your home well-structured with time management is a huge gift to a child, whose demands and distractions increase each year.

- Keep in mind this idea, which I share frequently with parents and teachers: If they knew how to do it, they would. Again, they are not struggling in school or getting poor grades or causing social problems to irritate you. They would like it to be easier, too. Come at them with mercy – and a helpful, structured plan.

- For a child who is struggling academically in many subjects, start with one subject at a time. With your child, list the skills or requirements that he/she has mastered or knows. (i.e., "In Spelling we have a pre-test each Monday and then I have to write sentences with my words by Wednesday. I did that last week and still have to do it this week.") Resist the urge to point out what they didn't do and scaffold the small success toward more consistent achievement.

- A common intervention to help disorganized students and to increase the family and school partnership is a Weekly Progress Check, or a daily sign-off on a planner or agenda. All teachers are willing to do this to support a child's success. (*See below for a sample I use in my school and adapt as fits your child.)

- Make a success chart where they are rewarded for completing work, but also for KNOWING and being honest about work not completed. For every test they bring home and show you, add points to the chart, not for the grade, but for the honesty of bringing home an assessment. This would also be true for the completed Weekly Progress Check, whether or not work is noted as missing. Bringing things home, communicating and bravely sharing, even when they slip up, is the way parents will get more honesty and more opportunity to scaffold their children with skills.

- Take the lead in communication with the teacher ALWAYS. Often, I hear parents bemoaning that the teacher should let them know when their child has not turned in work. But remember, that is not their responsibility; they have 180 versus your one. Additionally, current technology allows for most of the grading to be accessible and transparent, with school websites providing homework information. However, if you have done your early relationship work, getting more communication is easy. Take a proactive, versus reactive, stance and seek information weekly or bi-monthly depending on the tendencies and struggles of your own child.

- Be in the habit, as I have shared before, of asking your children what they did turn in, got credit for, or were assigned, versus what wasn't turned in. Then lead with the assumption: "What is on the plate tonight?" Avoid the "Do you have any homework?" question which can set kids up for a quick closed answer. Assume they do and help them break it down.

- Rather than blaming a child for not turning something in that he or she completed, consider the same gift of mercy you offer others: He/she is well-intentioned, just not so skilled.

- Reward success and make a plan for more of it.

Samples of Support Tools

On the last pages of this chapter are two forms I have created and tweaked over the years to build and support success for my students. The Weekly Progress Check is a great communication tool that places responsibility, as well as opportunity for reward, on your student's shoulders. The student, not the parent, bring this form to their subject teachers. In elementary, where they often have just one or two teachers, you can change the form and ask for just one signature. The child should bring this form around each Thursday (with his or her name, current week being evaluated, and subjects written in prior to giving it to the teacher). This allows a full day for the teacher to return it to the student who brings it home to you on Friday. Again: with any new habit, lots of support and reminding will be needed for everyone – you, teacher, and child! (Alternatively, a daily sign-off on a planner works well if parents consistently ask to see it.)

Give recognition and privileges for bringing it back to you signed and with the information needed to take care of any missing pieces. This is where the big full-on positive attention is paid, rather than on the missing links. As your child experiences positive relationship about being responsible to bring the signed paper home, he/she will avoid it less, be honest more often. And if you are over the moon about his or her having no outstanding work in one class, the child will work to see more of that in all their classes. Small steps build toward the big ones here, so working to create a habit of good communication, organization, and honesty is the initial objective. (Note: often the decision and buy-in around using Weekly Progress Checks and/or daily sign-off of the student planner is a direct result of the student success meeting.)

The second form is simply something you could adapt for use in a family **Student Success Meeting**. Or take the form into the school and set one up for your child. This is the best kind of advocacy, taking the lead on scaffolding your child's success choices from the start.

WEEKLY PROGRESS CHECK

My Name _____ Homeroom _____

For the week of _____

I would like to gain better control of my responsibilities as a student at _____ School. Could you please complete the following few questions? (My weekend may depend upon it! ☺)

Subject: _____

Teacher signature: _____

My focus in class has been: + 4   3   2   1 -

All assignments were handed in?   Yes / No

Missing Assignments: _____

_____

Upcoming assignment or tests: _____

_____

Recently graded assignments: _____

_____

COMMENTS:

(Duplicate above form for additional subjects.)

STUDENT SUCCESS MEETING

Student Name _____ Grade ____

Date: _____

Parents/Guardians attending:

_____

Teachers/Staff present (subjects):

_____

_____

Student's Qualities of Greatness (i.e., strengths and skills as a student such as motivation, persistence, respect, etc.):

Goals for Success (i.e. turn in major project, complete daily math assignment, ask more questions, etc.):

Specific Plan for Achieving Goal connected to student's strength/skill (Goal: using planner daily. Existing strengths: motivation, persistence, strong communication, etc.)

Running a Parent Group:
No Whining Aloud or Allowed!

By the time parents find my website, email me, or give me a call, they have tried many other options. They have read other books and tried other systems. They have found themselves so deeply down the path of negative energy that they are now fearful that they have ruined the relationship future with their child. They are fearful, too, that their child will never learn to color within the lines of society's expectations. They start the conversation with a panicked listing of all the problems, taking full blame, and still so clearly in love with the great glimpses of greatness their child exhibits. Over the years, as I connect and coach many families, I find their feeling of isolation significant. No one else knows how much they struggle; no one else has a child equally challenging. You can imagine the relief and shared joy they experience (ironically) in learning that many other parents have struggled with defiance, disobedience, hitting, stealing, lying, tantrums, violent episodes, and dangerous behaviors. A parent group, because it is Nurtured Heart–based, is different from many other groups. We do not begin by going around in a circle complaining and sharing our most ghastly stories reflecting the weaknesses of our children. It is not therapy, nor is it, as I experienced in couple's counseling, focused on loss, past mistakes, regrets, and troubles. Here is the crux of the difference: The Nurtured Heart Approach is about strengths. It is about what we do right: so we can do more of it. Certainly, everyone in the group already knows all there have struggled with their greatness and bringing out that same greatness in their children. No one is made to feel more powerful by miring deep into the muck of the mistakes and the pain of the past. No one seeks to add more labels to the situation. We all get it. Really. Parenting has been harder than we expected. The rewards have been fewer and somehow we arrived at a point that felt almost desperate. But we are not alone. And our kid is still alive – and so are we. And we are so much, much more than that.

So here are some caveats I set forth when we work in partnership to support our clear intention to bring the Nurtured Heart Approach into habit in our family.

- NO complaining about our children, our spouses, or anyone else, neither directly to them, nor to us, nor to others. You can have a complaint, a situation. But complaining, in and of itself, is defeating and problem-focused. (And remember, NHA likes rules that are clear.)

- Conversely, dedicate yourself to "brag" about your child in front of your child, within earshot, with your spouse and parents and friends and the siblings. Commit to see and name greatness.

- Come prepared each week to share a success story of your parenting (a time you only leaked a little negativity, a time you held firm to your strictness of rules, a time you proactively recognized your child just before he/she appeared to be moving to break a rule, a time you reset yourself or simply didn't let the angst of a broken rule become personal).

- Be willing to say great things about the risk-taking of every parent in the room. Be brave enough to do the same about to your own parenting. Work to let go of past mistakes you feel you may have made (Chapter 3 on the Parent Trap) and be fearless in being able to "reset" yourself daily when you find yourself heading in that direction.

- Accept your greatness. Live in the now and the next moment. Refuse to energize past mistakes, but always feel free to energize past success.

- Finally, we are ALL the experts. We are great, though not perfect. And by taking on the challenging situations with Nurtured Heart, we are made greater when we add our own personality into the solution-focused discussions. Believing you are great is absolutely critical to bringing it out in your kid. And in our parent success group, the ideas you share reflect that objective each time. The most successful parents in my groups are the ones who say, "Try this." Or "I did this." These parents are creative problem solvers, persistent learners, positive thinkers, risk-takers, clever schemers, and patient listeners. They can take responsibility, reset themselves, step away from energizing negativity, see themselves as capable, self-controlled and self-aware. These are the parents who step in to share – and raise kids who reflect these same qualities. Who wouldn't want that kid in their family? Who wouldn't want that parent?

Four to Six Week Group Format

There are many models out there for coaching parents in groups. All can be adapted to fit your style and audience. I find that having no more than ten parents in a group allows for each person to make a connection. I frequently have parents who attend as a couple but often have them work with another parent during some of the activities that are done in pairs. This helps give a voice to each parent independently You will find that with couples someone usually takes the lead in introductions or stories, and the group can miss out on a different perspective of that same child or situation.

I do not require that my parents have any Nurtured Heart background; I ask simply that they are motivated to learn and participate. Who doesn't want to be a successful parent, stepping into life's greatest role? I also do not require spouses to attend, though I love it when both are on board. I have found that my groups have pulled in a rich diversity of parenting styles and backgrounds that enhance the connection. I have been able to offer childcare in different locations for my groups, which greatly enhances the possibility of having both partners attend. I also have had more success when I offer my classes on a Sunday around the noon hour. I generally bring copies of Glasser's books to sell or recommend. Both *All Children Flourishing: Igniting the Greatness of Our Children* (c. 2009) and one co-authored with gifted Nurtured Heart Trainer Lisa Bravo, *Transforming the Difficult Child Workbook: An Interactive Guide to the Nurtured Heart Approach* (c. 2008) are great support tools for parents to have at home for deeper understanding and practice. (Of course, the book you hold in your hand is a perfect tool, too!)

I also provide handouts, which give the basic principles and perspectives of NHA, available on my website at www.nurturedheart.net, and adjective cards with long lists of words of greatness as a resource for us to use when we are working to build our own vocabulary of qualities of greatness. My current list, available in the appendices, was actually created by one of my parent groups in a brainstorm activity. (This is something you can do the second week in your group.) Typing that up and distributing it the next week gives them not only a tangible, personalized tool that they can use, but it is also something with which they can take personal ownership, seeing concrete evidence of their <u>own</u> greatness.

Each week, end your session with an assignment. Perhaps it is energizing your spouse daily. Perhaps, it is going back and recalling a success story and bragging about your child to your child. Or maybe it is trying one of the adjective games (ideas in Chapter 9) or presenting the system of relationship to your family. Start a family meeting. Decide not to complain. Call your spouse/in-laws/sister/best friend and brag about what your child did. Explain your system to another significant adult who knows your child, like the parent of one of his/her good friends. Bring a successful parent story where the parent reset him/herself, did not give a warning, was strict to rules, or remembered to energize what was going right in a difficult moment.

Generally sessions flow easily with dialogue, supportive laughter, teary stories of difficult moments, and deep revelations of love for children. You can always have springboard Parent Group Questions or Common Parent Dilemmas ready. (Examples of both are at the end of this chapter.) Cut these in strips and pass them out randomly to answer individually or in partners and then share as a whole group to allow all to give feedback. The dilemmas are also fun to act out for the parents because it provides more verbal practice, and allows for us to step into our child's shoes with intentional thought.

Week 1: Introduction and Overview of NHA

Create a safe place for parents to share by opening up with your own stories and introduction. Lay the ground rules (see above) that keep the conversation solution-focused, versus exhaustive complaining. Energize the parents for what it takes each day to bring the best version, especially a committed version, of themselves in relationship with a challenging child. Participants can make name tags for the table so that they can be used each time. Each person should share a specific, personal goal and write it down. These can be weekly. Give an overview of NHA using some of Glasser's good stories and analogies, or your own examples of what the three Stands of the approach look like in certain situations. Give the parent success assignment for the week.

Week 2: Focus on the First Stand: Absolute No! Energy to Negativity

Begin with the full-on decision to step away from being reactionary to triggers and energizing negativity.

As you reunite, review introductions and ask participants to share their parent success story. After each story, energize the parents by pointing out any time they were able to step away from a clearly negative situation. Help participants honor what it takes to be clear and not energize behaviors we are trying to extinguish. What does it say about parents when they do NOT respond to a child's defiance with matched negativity? Children who break rules irritate us. They are defiant and poorly mannered, right? Most parents, and quite honestly most people in relationship, are already experiencing this heavy burden. We complain. We argue. We whine. Our children complain. Our children argue. Our children whine. In fact, these darn kids hit, they disobey, they sulk. We get this. They get this. And so far, our traditional relationship responses are not working.

Beginning with this first Stand is both refreshing and challenging, too. Particularly challenging (in fact, this exists throughout your small group) is keeping the group focused on the next moment of success rather than on the litany of problems. How perfect is it to begin with this Stand: Absolute No! Use it firmly in the discussions in your group. Have a complaint (quick, specific and needing solution) but no complaining (ongoing, problem-focused, and negatively energized). Be firm with this and allow everyone to breath into it the real angst and struggle, but coach your parents to stop taking these broken rules personally. Additionally, help them to keep their reflective negative response in check internally until they become fully NHA-immersed. They will continue to feel the frustration, they just do not need to let their child see or be rewarded by the response. This is not about them in weakness. It is about them in Greatness.

At this point in your small group, most everyone will begin to relax and trust more. Honor each member for what it takes to come each week and what a powerful message this commitment sends to his or her family. Ask again what quality in their children they were trying to energize and build in the previous week. Turn the tables on them and energize them for that same quality. Cooperation: "Here, in our group you are demonstrating this quality right now, taking turns." Begin with a group or partner dilemma where the team has to come up with what could be going right when a child is having a tantrum, ignoring a request, or arguing with the parents over a rule or consequence. Let them get creative. (If your group is a six-week model, this activity can be extended each week into role-playing the parent responding in this difficult way.) Use other dilemmas from the handout at the end of this chapter, which call on a parent to step away from nagging, warning, and anger. Make it personal by asking each member to think of the time when it is particularly hard for him or her to step away from negatively energizing the relationship. Then let the group help them strategize ways to reset themselves or remove themselves. Ask them to share a time when they did just that, the hard thing. An appropriate assignment would be to focus on that common situation to intentionally not give negative energy (not arguing, defending, warning, or lecturing). Alternatively, give one of the questions or dilemmas to each member as a springboard to begin next session.

Week 3: Focus on the Second Stand: Absolute Yes: Energizing What Is Going Right

After reintroductions, brainstorm all the possible qualities of greatness that their children may demonstrate. Do this in partners. Make a large group list. Post and have it handy at future meetings. Share success stories and solutions to dilemmas in the larger group. After each story, honor each parent's courage, self-control, insight, and other skills he/she used in the situation (i.e., remaining calm, thinking ahead, respect, patience, intelligence, teamwork, humility, bravery, etc.). Return to the list of words. Participant should each select a characteristic that they do not normally associate with their child. Then ask them to think of a time that their child exhibited this quality. (Every parent can, if prompted.) Use this as a springboard: If the child can do it once, he/she can do it again. Give an assignment to look and name this quality and come with more examples next week. Have them write the quality on a 3 X 5 card or Post-it and put it where they can be reminded at home (the refrigerator door, the car dashboard, the dining table, etc.). Set the week ahead as the chosen Quality: for example, Tolerance Week, Self-Control Week, Time-Management Week, and so forth. Tell them to be prepared to celebrate on their return.

Week 4: Focus on the Third Stand: Absolute Clarity, Limits, and the Reset

Begin by modeling positive recognition and ask each member to turn to the next person and do the same. Read aloud a section from any Nurtured Heart book that explores the challenge and reward of Strictness to Rules (i.e., my paragraph exploring analogies in Chapter 5 or page 80–81 in *Notching Up*). Grounding group question: *How is the Nurtured Heart Approach consequence different from other consequences?* Discuss punishment versus consequence, timed-out and timed-in, and the ultimate goal of a consequence. Share examples of successful resets, "hijacked" resets and resets given without negative energy. Role-play introducing resets to your children or family in partners. Let members bring their own dilemmas on maintaining clarity and strictness (keeping focused on the solution – not the problem!); introduce a discussion about handling other significant adults in their children's lives who do not use NHA, leak negativity, or bend rules. (Read aloud portions of Chapter 8 on this common dilemma.)

Added Weeks:

You can see it would be easy to fill up sessions with role-playing, questions, energizing parents, and fielding "what if" dilemmas. The ultimate goal is to empower parents to realize they have all they need to handle their intensely wonderful child. Using any of the questions or dilemmas as group or partner trouble-shooting is a way to practice the skills, build confidence, and work collaboratively. During the weeks that I work with a group, I field email questions and often share columns or resources that come my way. Most importantly, the parent group takes on its own form of a family focused on what is going right. The goal is to bring that addictive habit back home.

PARENT GROUP QUESTIONS

1. What is the best thing about being a parent?

2. What is one of the biggest daily challenges you face as a parent?

3. If you could wave a wand and get your wish, what particular skill or attribute would you grant with greater success to yourself?

4. If you could wave a wand and get your wish, what particular skill or attribute would you grant with greater success to your spouse or partner?

5. If you could wave a wand and get your wish, what particular skill or attribute would you grant with greater success to your child/children?

6. Of all the parenting advice you have ever received, what are some of the best bits of advice that you try to keep in mind?

7. What are two things you do for yourself to take care of yourself, so you can take care of others? What is one thing you wish you had more time for?

8. As you understand more about the Nurtured Heart Approach, which Stand of the three (no negativity, consistent positive recognition, strictness/clarity to rules) Stands of the approach do you feel is the hardest to maintain? When do you find you are more successful with it?

9. As you understand more about the Nurtured Heart Approach, which Stand of the three (no negativity, consistent positive recognition, strictness/clarity to rules) Stands of the approach do you feel successful with most often? When is this Stand especially hard to maintain?

10. Visualize yourself mid-argument with your intense child. You recognize that you are leaking negativity. What could you say or do to halt the direction of this interaction and move it toward greater success for both of you?

11. You understand and have experienced success with your children using the Nurtured Heart Approach. Your mother-in-law, however, doles out a lot of negative energy to your child over a broken rule and expects long time-outs or spanking. How can you address this challenging situation with both her and your child?

12. Armed with the knowledge of NHA and able to go back in time, how might you now handle a past situation with your child or partner that might build capacity more greatly, keep the focus firmly on what is going right or the next moment of success?

PARENT DILEMMAS: Holding Firm the Stands of Nurtured Heart

1. It is bedtime – a battle that can be hard won. How could you set it up for success prior to engagement in a negative battle? If your child complains, how could you use the Stands of the Nurtured Heart to gain compliance – and build capability?

2. Your child spends nearly every recess inside completing homework. The child still does not get it all done. It is beginning to alter how he/she views school, the teacher, and his/her own ability. How can you derail the negative direction of the situation? What conversations might you have with the child and/or the teacher?

3. Your child's room is a disaster of toys and clothes and disorganization. You have set a rule that he cannot go to the movie until his room is cleaned. It is 20 minutes before it is time to leave. You peek into the room and see that he has only made his bed, and the rest of the requests have not been done. What do you say? What do you do?

4. You have a rule of no television after 8:00 p.m. Your child whines every time you turn the television off at night. It exhausts you. Using the Stands of the Nurtured Heart Approach, how can you scaffold her to successfully handle this family rule and keep yourself focused on what is going right?

5. You have friends coming for dinner. Nearly every time you have people over, your children seem to ramp up their need for attention. They interrupt, they refuse to clean up after themselves, they argue. You often let rules slide because it can be so embarrassing. How can you set it up for success? How do you respond when they argue in front of your friends?

6. Your child complains frequently about a friend at school who is mean to her. Each day she shares another story of being made fun of, left out, or teased. It breaks your heart. You have tried to get her to play with other kids, but she seems to be drawn to this girl. What do you say?

7. Your child seems to do fine in school, makes friends, and gets along with others. When he gets home, however, he is cranky and complains a lot. He picks fights with his siblings and argues. How can you address this proactively?

8. The coach on your child's soccer team does a lot of "comparison" comments, leaking negativity, or using sarcasm to motivate other kids. Your child does not handle this well, and tends to shut down, take in the negative energy, and get discouraged. How could you address this with your child and/or the coach?

9. In the parking lot or bus stop, one parent in particular is very negative about another child, labeling her as a bully or mean girl. Your own daughter has complained about this child, but you find this kind of conversation neither productive nor empowering to the child. What are some ways to use the approach on this parent? Is it possible or appropriate to use the approach on this other girl, too?

10. Someone observes you using the Nurtured Heart Approach with your children during a play date. They are intrigued. Create a 30-second "elevator speech" that explains the approach from your own personal voice and intention.

How to Coach Other Significant Adults in Your Child's Life

Becoming Fluent

A funny thing happens when you begin to live your life armed with the Nurtured Heart Approach; you mentally translate all relationships around you in NHA. I do not mean to imply that you sit in judgment, criticizing and focusing on parent interactions that do not measure up to your standards. It is as though your eyes are more open to recognizing non–Nurtured Heart choices as you process alternate ways of responding in parenting situations. In the grocery store, you see a frustrated parent grab her child roughly away from the candy. You hear a grandparent threaten a child with a spanking. You observe parents yelling at an already crying child, with the futile demand, "Stop crying!" And while you, yourself, may also slip into this negative energizing when you are under stress, your lens has shifted significantly. You see a different way that removes all the intense negative response and relationship.

In many ways, I think of it like learning a foreign language. At first the words don't come easily; the grammar is wrong and the vocabulary limited. Then, as with most things we must practice to master, it begins to come naturally. We think in the foreign language. We translate, perhaps still with some stilted phrasing, the language of NHA into our relationships. We are approaching fluency! The advantage of parent groups and working with others who understand the language and constructs of NHA is that it helps us move toward fluency, toward more easily resetting ourselves, forgiving ourselves and our children when any of us "break a rule" or energize a poor choice. I love watching this happen as I work with parents. They hit pause, a simple reset option, and they translate the moment into an opportunity to build success. I will share a story that illustrates what I mean.

At the coffee shop, I was standing in line with one of these nearly fluent NHA parents. A small boy, probably about four-years-old, was gazing up at the long row of alluring pastries, tugging his mother's hand and whining clearly that he "wanted one." First, let's all agree that this marketing of fluffy breads, sugar-coated donuts, and fruit-filled concoctions is torture for each of us and tests our <u>own</u>, more mature self-control; understandably, this poor boy simply succumbed to its proximity. His well-intentioned mother grabbed his hand back and firmly said, "No! You know what I said." He whined a bit louder. And added the tortured moan of "Whhhyyyyy???" (See section on "Because I Said So" in Chapter 11: *Creative Strategies to Bringing NHA into Habit.*)

Let's also acknowledge that while it is incredibly annoying to have a child whine and plead and beg for things, the actual job of a child is to see life as abundance and choice. He is doing his literal developmental job. Any parent can relate to this moment. But to be fair, she is setting boundaries. Being firm. Being consistent. And he is testing the boundary. The child has not willingly let go of the possibility that his persistence may pay off. Perhaps it has worked before. (We, too, admit we have given into the repeated, painful pleas of our begging children, especially in public, with the hopes of ending an uncomfortable escalation.) We see it could get worse for either the mom or the child. We mentally fast-forward to her yanking him out of line and leaving the store, raising her voice, to the boy losing self-control and hitting her leg, starting a tantrum, loudly debating the reasons for and against this denial of treat, and so on.

This is where we wince a bit in fearful anticipation – and where this amazingly fluent speaker of NHA steps in to gracefully reset the course of this interaction. She bends down near the child and matches his gaze at the tempting donuts above. "You are so right. Those all look so good, don't they. Wow! You are listening so well to your mom. I can tell it is hard. I am so impressed with you!" (I assure you, I am not making this up!) She pauses and smiles reassuringly up at the mom who is frozen but primed for battle. "I don't think my son would be as patient," she adds, kindly. The mom takes in what Howard Glasser would call this "hijack" to Greatness, and meets her gaze with relief. The boy is surprised, perhaps wondering, "Who is this big stranger?" But then he smiles at her shyly. He moves to press against his mom's leg and takes her hand. Now this is where this hijacking pays off: the mom of the now patient four-year-old doesn't miss a beat. "He really does listen well, doesn't he?" she praises. "Thank you, Hung, for remembering we have lots of treats at home." Hung, quite unsure what just happened, nods his head to her compliment.

BAM! Exasperated mom: reset to proud, capable mom. Little boy: energized for doing the hard thing. It was a fluid moment of knowing the right thing to say at the right time. It was fluency in choice of words, tone, and energy. It is what we seek as NHA practitioners. It is neither the easy thing, nor often the first thing we think to do. When we travel, our automatic default is to speak our own language. But the longer we are in the foreign country, the more habitual it becomes to speak the language of the new country. This scenario reminded me, too, that it is often much easier to see/know the right thing to say or do when you are not emotionally invested into the relationship. This four-year-old, Hung, was not pushing OUR buttons. He was not breaking a rule WE had set. (*"Now remember when mommy goes in to get coffee, we are not getting a treat today,"* she likely coached.) We were not worried, as she might have been, about what other parents might say or think.

In this way, it was easy for the NHA translator to step in without criticism or shame, and actually praise the boy, because we all know he could be behaving much worse, right? The mom also accepted the comment as positive recognition, even if it was distraction for the boy, and was able to reinforce it further. It was a gift of sorts to both boy and mom.

Certainly, I am not suggesting we intervene in every parental/child conflict as Nurtured Heart Relationship Super Heroes. (has a good ring to it, though). Minus the heart-shaped cape and red tights, we are just learning each day and each new moment how to see and name what is going right first. Knowing that this is hardest with those we love the most, why not practice on strangers or acquaintances? Practice frequently on the children of your friends. Practice naming what is going right when you are hanging out with your nieces, nephews, your sister or your in-laws. Practice with the cashier and the neighbor with the barking dog. Practice with the office staff and your book club. Plan what to say. Predict what might happen and hijack the moment with a positive recognition. Broaden and deepen your vocabulary; often one of the first walls we hit is running out of things to say in the spur of the moment. The safety of this kind of practice is brilliant. First off, you really can't mess up too badly when you are trying to name what is going right. Secondly, you can do it in baby steps because emotionally you are not as concerned with the push back. Finally, nearly every single person who receives a comment of his or her strengths accepts it. You model this kind of recognition – and they pay it forward. Win-win. BAM!

(See "Activity II" in Chapter 11: *Creative Strategies to Bringing NHA into Habit*)

Helping Others Name Greatness

I have worked with many parents (and grandparents, step-parents, childcare providers, teachers, girlfriends and other significant adults who serve in a parental role) who get the Nurtured Heart Approach at its core. While still working to keep the three Stands firm (naming what is going right, not energizing poor choices or negative consequences, and maintaining consistency to rules), their spouse/partner/live-in parent has not bought into the power of NHA. They leak negativity (actually, sometimes flood it!); they step in and energize poor choices by lecturing, scolding, spanking, and yelling. They threaten consequences but never deliver. They waver and say, "Next time." They bully the child with threats of violence or over-the-top consequences ("He actually said to him, 'I am going to burn that television,'" one frustrated mom shared with me. "Like we were ever going to burn the television!"). It is difficult not to get discouraged in situations like these. It is difficult to remain firm in your own practice; it is already hard not to slip into warnings yourself! Difficult, yes! Possible, yes!

Before we tackle some strategies for coaching the adults in our lives, I want to remind you of the greatness you are. When I was first trained as an Advanced Trainer in 2007, I was well-versed in NHA. I had read the book, attended the daylong workshop with Howard Glasser and begun practicing the system of relationship with my own children and students. What I learned in that powerful week, however, is that in order to use the system – I had to BE the system myself. I had to see and name greatness in myself. I could not begin to be powerfully transformative in the lives of the children I worked with if I did not allow this in myself. This shift came most powerfully during my second day of the training when we sat in smaller groups of parents, therapists and educators and worked on energizing each other, despite being nearly strangers. Even the most reticent participant was able to see strengths in those around him/her. Silence could mean wisdom and clarity. Eye-contact indicated compassion, strong listening, and patience. Laughter demonstrated engagement and empathy.

One brave stranger, a wonderful, dedicated adoptive mom, shared that in her whole life she had felt that she had been "too much." Her husband had told her that in many ways. Her friends had indicated it repeatedly. It was a powerful moment for all of us, because when we open to hear someone else's truth, we own a piece of it ourselves. Too much? Yes. We can relate. I could relate. I was too loud. Too opinionated. Too eager. Too verbal. Too direct. Too antsy. Too much. The conversation flowed to another individual who ironically shared that he had felt so much the opposite, "not enough." Oh yes. We could relate, too. I could relate. I was not enough of an organizer. Not enough of a person who could forgive. Not enough of a parent, because I liked to be without my kids sometimes. I was not enough of a homeowner or employee because I liked to play more than work. Not enough. So, in the company of strangers, we made this powerful connection that this greatness we must name in others and work to become: WE ALREADY ARE! We are not perfection, nor are we seeking this in others. We are seeking greatness and naming it in ourselves. We cannot begin to empower others if we do not allow ourselves the same luxury of imperfect greatness acknowledged. In that transforming hour, I began to own my imperfect greatness. I got it: I was too much and not enough and just right. And so are you. By the sheer nature of you picking up this book and reading these lines, you can no longer deny it. Now, when I coach my students, I always tell them, "I am not perfect, but I AM great. Are you perfect?" I ask the students. "No way," they smile. "Are you great?" "Absolutely!" they laugh.

So from this point onward, when you feel the approach failing you, when you go to self-criticism and negative complaining, you must reset yourself to focus on what you are doing right. Remember Yoda's famous line from *Star Wars*, "Do or do not. There is no try." Forget that. The line misses its mark because in simple act of trying to name greatness, you are becoming that greatness. Done! Now, armed with this knowledge of your imperfected greatness, you are reminded of another point. You are powerful, even as just one. When you hit the wall of disbelief in relation to others around you who flood negativity and are unskilled in naming greatness, you must remember YOU ARE SKILLED. You cannot protect your child from all the other significant adults in his/her world who will choose to criticize, humiliate, or bully. I wish you could. I wish we could make everyone be nice, right? Given our reality, we can only control our OWN attitudes and choices. And this, in itself, is a powerful piece of knowledge.

I have often coached my students with this same idea. They come in to complain about a mean kid on the playground or a friend who seemed to suddenly turn on them. It's sad, I know. But here, my goal is to help them shift the focus. The child's awareness of his or her greatness is the only tool that can empower him/her in that common situation. While we might wish we could remove our children from those mean kids and unkind adults, our real role as *Nurtured Heart Relationship Super Heroes* is to build their inner wealth and resiliency. People, all their life actually, will say and do unkind things. They will get hurt and will want to hurt back. It is that latter part (their attitude, response, and download of messages) that NHA greatness can counter. We can't change people, but people CAN change.

So while you cannot place your child in the bubble of only kindness, you can become the greatest gift they have in their world. You cannot control the responses of any other person; however, you are in control of your own. You are building the inner wealth of your children daily; you are coaching them that they are capable of handling all of life's challenges, including difficult people who love them. You are powerfully great in this role, and for most situations, YOU ARE ENOUGH. While our ultimate goal is to get all the adults in our children's world to see and name our children's greatness, to see their own greatness and potential, to see the world as abundance, we can only, as Mahatma Gandhi so eloquently reminded us, "Be the change we wish to see in the world." Shift your lens, as you coach your child to handle negative people, negative words, and cruel comments, to remain focused on what is going right and on your own choice, each day, to be this change. You can help your child see, as you yourself are learning to see, that nearly all people are well intentioned. The significant adults in your children's world want them to be successful, but perhaps lack some of the tools to support them toward that goal positively. You are just enough to be this change.

You begin to see how powerful your intention is when it must go beyond your own child, and work to bring out the best version of all the adults working with your child. Your own lens needs to be one that focuses on this greatness in every human being, even the most challenged. When you consider a challenged child, one who struggles to stay within the lines, the Nurtured Heart Approach calls us to compassion. The child doesn't break the boundaries to anger you. He is learning. He wants to connect and belong. But he is unskilled. If our goal is to coach this child toward his great capacity, then we know we must stay firm in the belief that he CAN do it. We have learned to show the child this evidence repeatedly. Here you are being patient. Here you are showing self-control, respect, responsibility, teamwork. Right? You got this. You are building the inner wealth of that child, and the reward to your diligence is his ultimate independence, success in relationships, and confidence in the challenges of life.

Now consider this adult who also struggles. Take a minute and see him or her as a similar child who has yet to truly discover his or her greatness. She has habits of relationship built on years of downloaded messages of negativity. Does she want the child to love her? To respect her? To be successful and make good choices? Yes, of course. This adult is well-intentioned, and much like the child, UNSKILLED.

This may come across as arrogant, this approach of seeing the adult as a person to coach, as you would a child. But it is a powerful paradigm shift to see this adult as CAPABLE, in the same way you see your children as capable of following all the rules/expectations you set forth to train them toward independence. When a significant adult in your child's life does not yet understand the power of parenting with the Nurtured Heart Approach, you must turn that approach on them. You must be relentless and fearless in naming this partner's greatness, her intention, her commitment. And you must start small.

Here are some of the common responses, shared by parents seeking help with other well-intentioned adults, which reflect a clash with NHA.

> *"That's it? He gets a 'reset" and then he can go back out and play?"*

> *"He needs to learn to listen. You need to discipline him."*

> *"He must be consequenced. Just give him a spanking."*

Worse yet, they turn to the child.

> *"You are a naughty, naughty girl."*

And so on. Then these well-intentioned adults step in with actions: The child is sent to her room for an entire afternoon.

All her toys are removed all day. She receives a long lecture and a barrage of negative statements about her character and disrespectful attitude. She is shamed and scolded, slapped and excluded from life. She is threatened with unreasonable and undeliverable consequences: "We are going to leave the store." "You will not get to play with your cousins again." "No one will ever want to come over to our house again." "I am not buying you another coat for the rest of the year."

Naming the Greatness of "Difficult Adults"

Phew! Even that level of adult anger and energy around a child's behavior feels like bullying. And when we aren't firm in our own greatness, it is easy to take in these reactions as criticism of our parenting style. We could leak negativity back: Accuse the adult of bullying or mishandling a situation, become defensive and aggressively explain our method, say nothing but harbor resentment. But if our ultimate intention is pure: To name what is going right with our child, to remain firm and unemotional with our expectations, then we need to do the same with this adult. The adult does not agree with (nor understand) our parenting system; to defend it in the moment of anger or frustration so rarely works. The lens of the well-meaning adult is honed on his/her own default of how to raise a child, and this default feels the polar opposite of your approach. So how DO you respond? You take control of the emotional moment by taking the lens off the adult's response to the child's misbehavior. You fire right back with the ADULT'S greatness and capability. You avoid criticism of the way the adult handled the situation, because criticism is rarely heard as constructive and generally creates more barriers in a healthy relationship. You step into your own greatness and become fearless in seeing and naming what is going right for that adult; you soften this impasse by turning the approach right on to the very person who needs it the most at that moment.

Quick. Review the way you have practiced naming what could be going right when a child is having a tantrum: she is showing strong emotion, she is angry but not hitting, she is using her words which shows she is very intelligent and also working to calm herself down, she has strong opinions and is a risk-taker, she is passionate and dedicated, SHE IS WELL-INTENTIONED, etc. Now take a minute to consider what qualities are demonstrated by a grandparent or other adult who disciplines differently? She is... She could be... but she is.... She is...Try this on your own. Really see the adult as well meaning but unskilled. See the adult as another person seeking to make and keep relationship; see the adult's own fear as a driving force in the often negative response; see the adult as a child who missed out having his/her capabilities named. Flood your head with these capabilities right now. (You can see a list of positive qualities that this adult could be exhibiting in the appendices, though by now I imagine you are getting very good at this!) Do this mentally before you begin verbally with the adult.

What we have demonstrated again and again when it comes to naming what is going right is this: You get more of whatever you name. You want more patience. Name it. You want more matched consequences with actions. Name it.

"Granddad, I can tell you were frustrated with Eloisa when she didn't seem to be listening. I thought it was so great that you looked her in the eye and were calm. You are so patient. It could be easy to yell in that moment. I have lots to learn from you."

I often hear disbelieving parents say that this is dishonest. "Granddad is not patient!" they contend. Shift your lens and let yourself remember even a small moment of time when "Granddad" was patient. Nearly, everyone is able to conjure a Granddad memory. (Sidebar note to parent: I use this same trick of the lens when a parent is struggling with his or her own child. "You want Conner to show more respect? Name a time or situation from the past when Conner demonstrated respect? Self-control? Responsibility?" or any of the qualities the parent wishes he or she saw demonstrated more frequently. Once you can see your children exhibiting the quality you are seeking, it becomes a more manageable obstacle to see them as capable of this quality more and more.)

Decide to see "Granddad" as patient. Decide to stop complaining about when he is impatient. Decide to hijack every moment where patience could be lost and honor the small step. Finally, decide to only energize what you want more of. Then step away from discussions, lectures, defensive standoffs, or any other non-productive communication that does not build the capacity of this adult to see him or herself as patient, tolerant, understanding, and so forth. I counter that most adults spend a majority of their lives not being noticed when they, too, do the hard thing. The act of a simple recognition has great power to open up the lines of communication and compassion. Consider the adult resisting your accusation of their greatness. Be fully armed with your own insistence, but keep it genuine and simple.

I remember one mom sharing her attempt at this with her mom, whom she depended on for childcare when she went to work. "I just would not tolerate the smart mouth from him, Doreen." Her mother met her at the door complaining loudly, clearly frustrated and feeling disrespected by her grandson. NHA Super Mom, "You work so hard to help him understand your expectations, Mom. I don't know what I would do without your calm presence when he isn't being so calm himself," she hijacked. Bam! Complimented and recognized, it was far easier for her to become the person her daughter was recognizing – calm and courageous. At the same time, NHA Super Mom needed her mom to step away from escalating a problem by energizing it with lots of focus and negative attention. She knew her son could press the buttons of those he loved and needed. (She understood full well Glasser's analogy of the ToysRUs and parents/teachers/siblings/caregivers being a child's favorite toy to wind up and get active!) NHA Mom had to refuse to go down that path herself daily! Her decision to empathize with her mom's frustration, and leave out any "buts" made the bridge to communication more open. (Try this: Before you read on to how she handled it next, consider what you could say in the same instance which would propel this grandparent further into her greatness and capacity to coach and manage the relationship with her grandson...)

Did you guess that she would continue to acknowledge, that yes, it is hard. That she would distract her mom from the complaints and problems, by actually changing the subject to what went well. It could have been worse. A fan of spanking in earlier years, Grandmom could have hit the boy; she could have been mid-tirade when mom got home. What else could NHA Mom energize? What else was going right? "Sounds like your quick reset of Bradley to his room worked like a charm, Mom. I don't hear a peep. He sounds very calm. He must really respect you when he follows your direction like that." NHA Mom reported to me that her mom grumbled a bit under her breath and then grudgingly admitted that he did go to his room for his time-out. "He slammed the door. though!" she protested weakly. NHA Mom actually laughed out loud and encouraged her mom to do the same. "I bet!" she acknowledged. "You let him know he needed to reset. So I guess he did." They were both chuckling. "I think he probably is way over the issue now, Mom. And you already are, because of course he is just the kid, and you know so much better than he does about how to reset yourself."

NHA Mom used the chance to slide in coaching with questions. She got her mom to name some things that went well that day, and when Bradley emerged, still a bit disgruntled from his room, she modeled for her mom how to welcome someone back to timed-life, without adding negative energy but honoring the good choice. "Bradley, you are so calm now. Grandma said she gave you a reset to your room and you went on your own without her having to take you. Grandma really was proud of how you accepted responsibility. You showed a lot of respect for yourself and for Grandma in that moment, even though it was hard." Bradley was used to this recognition from his mom. He knew his mom was disappointed, but she didn't focus on this and therefore, by doing this, she did not allow Grandma to do that either. Bradley apologized sincerely to his grandma. At first, out of a deep habit of needing to justify her actions, she began to re-educate Bradley around the expectations. NHA Mom graciously inserted herself. "Bradley, that was honorable that you recognized that your behavior hurt Grandma. She was angry, too. But she reset herself just like you did. I think you may want to think of a way to make amends."

Creative Strategies to Bring NHA into Habit

1. Because I Said So: This is Me Practicing Being Relentless

Both the inane question, "Why?" and the even sillier battle-cry response, *"Because I said so,"* are great reminders of the power of holding firm the Stands of the Nurtured Heart Approach. When we get defensive about our rules, we wiggle and leak negativity. Explaining why you are making a request or doling a consequence creates a shift in relationship that focuses on the problem. At the same time, clarity is so critical. If your rules are clear, and just as important, consistently followed without the backfire of the "next time" threat, then the battle zone of defensive volleying is cut short.

One of my favorite educational and parent consultants, Dr. Jane Bluestein, scaffolds Glasser's work when she outlines six solid reasons for avoiding the "why" debate. Bluestein recognizes keenly that spending time investigating around the "why" in a broken rule or poor choice puts our energy in the wrong direction.

Trying to find out why:

- Focuses on excuses rather than commitment.

- Assumes the child knows why he did it (or forgot) and can adequately explain his reasons.

- Suggests that your boundaries and limits are flexible if your children have a good enough excuse: "If you're creative (or pathetic) enough, you're off the hook."

- Puts you in the position of having to judge the validity of your children's excuses and arbitrarily decide whether or not to hold them accountable.

- May give you ammunition to attack or shame the child ("You should have thought of that before," "You should have known better," "How could you have been so stupid?"), instead of using the occasion as an opportunity for the child to make more responsible choices and correct his or her behavior.

- FINALLY: If you've got a good boundary with a positive outcome, if your children are developmentally able to do what you've asked and if they have had enough time, training, or reminders – AHEAD OF TIME versus in the moment or as a warning – to succeed, then WHY DOESN'T MATTER. The positive outcome is simply not available until the children change their behavior or fulfill their commitments. (This is full-on Nurtured Heart!)"[13]

It sounds so simple to say: "The rules are the rules." (Take just a minute and savor that concept.) The critical piece to this clarity really becomes much more about you as the parent holding firm to your expectation versus your child's developmental right to see if you really mean it. The challenge occurs at many levels, but let's simply take the most common in all developmental stages: Why?

Visualization Activity: This is Me Practicing Being Relentless

This is a great group activity with other parents as it can build skills and responses.

1. Think about a rule that you want your child to follow. (ex. pick up his/her clothes, clear the table, brush his/her teeth, turn off the electronics, etc.). Consider why this is an important rule to you and your family. Make it a simple, specific rule and reason.

2. Imagine that you are presenting this rule to a child who doesn't want to follow the rule. Consider some of the reasons he/she may not want to follow this rule. Here you actually do anticipate the "why?" question, but our energy

---

[13] Excerpted and adapted *from The Parent's Little Book of Lists: Do's & Don'ts of Effective Parent*ing by Dr. Jane Bluestein, © 1997, Health Communications, Inc., Deerfield Beach, FL.

is directed much more powerfully to the capacity to follow the request and the skills the child demonstrates by agreeing to complete the task.

3. Now imagine that you feel confident that the child will eventually follow the rule. It may not be in your immediate timeline or with the glee that you desire. (See you, yourself, hopping up gleefully to wash a stack of dishes, if this vision can provide empathy for the task required.)

4. What can you say to support his/her good choice to follow the rule?

5. How can you best respond to a, "Why do I have to do that?" complaint?

6. Prior to the next predicted resistance, what could you say to scaffold for success in advance?

7. How can you remind yourself to not nag, lecture, or warn?

8. How can you use positive recognition when a child is NOT doing what you are asking?

These are great questions to actually bring to a family dinner conversation. Be transparent about your ultimate goal of family responsibility, teamwork, self-awareness, independence, and interdependence. Be equally transparent in advance about your expectations and the relevant "whys" behind your requests. By predicting some of the resistance and arming yourself with clarity, you are more able to remove defensiveness or frustration from your requests: "This family works best when we work as a team, and you are a key team player. I need you to..."

In response to question 8, I challenge you to consider this: When a child doesn't give us a reset, when a child won't do our simple requests or ignores our rules, look first to our leadership as the parent. When we try to be strict to rules and it smacks into the wall of defiance or refusal, it generally means we have failed to uphold those first Stands with integrity. Have we slipped away from flooding greatness? Are we consequencing with energetic relationship (anger, blame, and threats)? My experience tells me that this is often the case. Have we breathed in the miracle our child is lately? Have we appreciated their independent spirit and creative nature? "I love watching you so engaged in your Lego project, Ryan. That takes such focus and careful planning. We are washing our hands for dinner and coming to the table now. I need you to stop and join us, even though it is hard for you to do that. I hope you get to complete it later, but that is all up to you right now. If you come and set the table now, you will get to finish it later. If not, your Lego kit will have to be timed-out until tomorrow." Hijack the moment, if necessary. If Ryan looks at you, or even hesitates with his project: "Wow! You are moving to make the right choice, even though it is requiring so much self-discipline. I can't wait to tell your mom."

2. Building A Meaningful Word Bank: My NHA Version of Boggle™

Either independently, with your family members (as a NHA version of Boggle™) or as part of a group activity with other NHA strategists, take each of the following people and see how many different adjectives or phrases you can brainstorm which would name a "Quality of Greatness" in his or her actions, choices, attitudes, character or even non-actions. Allow only 20-30 seconds on the first round. If done as a group activity, write down all the words that each player brainstormed on a shared team paper. Do not include synonyms of the word "great" as these are automatic and do not name a defined quality or characteristic. For example: Great, Awesome, Terrific = Not enough, too general and abstract. Great with words, Awesome team player, Terrific at waiting = More specific and powerful.

If making a game out of it, each individual will score one point for any adjective/descriptor or positive phrase that no one else has named. This technique allows you to create a list of vocabulary which goes deeper than the first five words we use as our default (i.e., patient, respectful, responsible, compassionate, friendly, etc.) and makes it a fun way to creatively name greatness. You can put these categories on slips of paper or 3 X 5 cards and turn them over as a deck. Leave several blank or write, "Think of your own person/character." Alternatively, glance over this list and then make your own that focuses on your world specifically (individual names or relatives).

When you have a list of 100 words, personally select one or two to use each day so that the practice of naming greatness becomes a sustained habit of using strong and deep recognitions, which accurately name the actions or qualities you want to see more of.

NHA BOGGLE™ BRAINSTORM:

Draw a "person" from the pile, and in 30 seconds name as many positive qualities as you can to describe the skills and abilities of this person. Spelling doesn't count (until we move it to the posted family list!). Note: younger players can shout word out and have older players write it down. ➔

POLICEMAN PULLING YOU OVER	GROCERY STORE BAGGER
NEIGHBOR WITH A BARKING DOG	HOMELESS MAN BEGGING
BARISTA (COFFEE SERVER)	CHILD SITTING IN CHURCH
A TEENAGER WITH PIERCING	BUS DRIVER
YOUTH GROUP LEADER	CUSTOMER SERVICE REP ON PHONE
RECEPTIONIST AT FRONT DESK	BANK TELLER
	LANDSCAPE WORKER
DENTAL HYGIENIST WORKING ON YOUR TEETH	PERSON WORKING ON COMPUTER IN COFFEE SHOP
PARENT WATCHING HIS CHILD PLAY IN SOCCER GAME	TABLE BUSSER IN A BUSY RESTAURANT
PLAYGROUND SUPERVISOR	YOUR CHILD'S BEST FRIEND
NATIONALLY RECOGNIZED SPEAKER	ACQUAINTANCE WHO GREETS YOU IN MALL

STRANGER'S CHILD
WHINING IN LINE
FOR CANDY

HOSTESS FOR A
HOLIDAY PARTY

NURSE TAKING
YOUR DATA

ONE OF YOUR BEST
FRIEND'S MOMS

PET GROOMER

SPORTS FAN NEXT
TO YOU AT THE
STADIUM

YOUR MOST
DISTANT SIBLING

YOUR CLOSEST
AUNT/UNCLE

GOOD FRIEND'S
DEFIANT CHILD

CO-WORKER WHO
LIKES TO TALK

THE DRIVER WHO
HONKS

THE YOUTH COACH
WHO YELLS OFTEN

YOUR CHILD'S
TEACHER

A GRANDPARENT
WHO FORGETS

DRIVER ON HIS
CELL PHONE

THE TELE-
MARKETER

THE VALET

GIRL SCOUT COOKIE
MOM

PTSA OFFICER AT
THE LOCAL SCHOOL

THE HOURLY
EMPLOYEE WAVING
THE STORE SIGN

THE EMPLOYEE AT
THE GOODWILL
TRUCK WHO
ACCEPTS YOUR
DONATION

3. The Adjective Game: Some Ways to Make It PERSONAL

One brilliant parent practitioner, whom I was honored to have in several of my parent small groups, created a fabulous, original tool to add to her son's nighttime routine. She took a shoebox and covered it with plain paper. Then she took a long list of positive adjectives from one of Glasser's books, wrote them on small pieces of construction paper and put them in the box. Each night, she would sit with her son and they would pull a paper out of the box and read the word together: PATIENCE or RESILENCE or FORGIVING and so on. Her goal was to help build her son's ownership of his greatness and capability (Glasser names this resilient term: Inner Wealth[14]). Her goal was also to reset both of them after what might have been a challenging day of drawn battle lines. "Okay, when do you think you showed patience today, Myles?" "When did you think you saw Mommy showing patience today?" "How about at school?" And the brilliant mommy would add lots of other times she saw this demonstrated, even if her own patience had been tried repeatedly. She was persistent and kept up the game for many months. After the word was taken from the box and talked about, they glued the word to the outside of his **GREATNESS BOX.** "These are Myles's Qualities of Greatness for all to see!" Then, as the adjectives grew to as

---

[14] *The Inner Wealth Initiative: The Nurtured Heart Approach for Educators* by Tom Grove and Howard Glasser (c. 2007)

many inside as outside, they would read ones outside and revisit them on a new day with newer tales of greatness.

I loved hearing this creative mom share an idea and watch as other parents ran with it and adapted it to their bedtime routine. One brave and persistent parent decided to step out of the battle zone of her child's desire to draw on the wall. She simply modified the rule. The wall above her son's bed became Jason's Wall of Fame, and she allowed her son, with her guidance, to write selected adjectives that they could build and talk about each night. Sometimes she used his Wall of Fame as a way to welcome him back from a reset, rereading a word of his greatness that he demonstrated when he accepted his reset responsibly. Soon, the son wanted to add pictures reflecting his greatness, and best of all, it became their private term ("I am thinking of the ??Myle's Wall of Fame," she would say) to refocus him if he began to move in the wrong direction. How much more powerful is a Wall of Fame than a Hall of Shame.

As I mentioned in an earlier chapter, the **Dinner Table Game** is another way to get in the habit of naming what is going right. Alternatively, you can take a brainstormed list of Q.O.G.'s (Qualities of Greatness) available in the appendices sor in any of Glasser's books and put them on 3 x 5 cards or strips of paper. Keep them in a basket and pass them around the dinner table, picking out one card either per person or one per night. Here you play as a family and each family member gets a chance to be in the **Greatness Hot Seat**. Place all the adjectives drawn up on the table so everyone can see them. The first the first few times you play the game, have an adult begin so that the habit of going overboard on greatness is established. The adult will look at either the one family word (i.e., KIND) or the group of words (i.e., KIND, HELPFUL, TRUTHFUL, PATIENT, for example). He/she will start with one person and name examples of times they have seen this family member demonstrate the Q.O.G. anytime that week.

> *"I am going to start with Alice. Alice demonstrated kindness when she came to the table for dinner right away. She was helpful when she took things out to the table for me and was also very helpful when she picked up her shoes from the entryway. When I was on the phone with a client, she was so patient, especially because I know she wanted to ask me something, but she had to wait. Ummmm... let's see...Truthful, oh yes... when I asked Alice to pick up her shoes and she didn't say she already picked them up, but headed right over to do it. I so appreciated that you were truthful, Alice."*

In this style, other people can now add more examples of Alice demonstrating the Q.O.G. and most family members have little trouble coming up with at least another example, as they are often eager for it to be his or her turn soon. As the adult, you can use positive recognition on those who are energizing, too. Being able to see and name something positive about your sibling or parent, especially when there had likely been some previous disagreement, is definitely something you want to energize as greatness. Initially, as you play any version of this game, buy-in is fairly high and the cooperation you get outside of the Dinner Table Game naturally goes up a bit. Kids and spouses now realize that their behaviors can be celebrated in a more formal way and they will seek this out.

Another adaptation to this activity is to be intentional about the qualities you want to build more of and simply make it a **Word of the Week**. Stay focused on that word and tell family members in advance what you will be celebrating and naming during the Greatness Hot Seat Game. "Today's word is TIME MANAGEMENT. Everybody try to pay attention to all the good examples we see each other demonstrate of good time management." On some words, you may need to define it or be specific about behaviors. This is such a great way to build a working vocabulary, and lens, on greatness. Even small children can learn big words like INTEGRITY and SELF-DISCIPLINE. Once they understand the word and the behaviors that demonstrate this characteristic, it becomes much easier to build more of it.

Finally, as I shared in the chapter on running a parent group, you can actually create your own family list of words independent of other lists. Brainstorm at the table, add words every time you see them, keep a running list on large paper that you can add to, and finally, after many weeks of building it, type it up, laminate it, and post copies everywhere.

Things That Make You Go Hmm....
Some Other Thoughts on Fearless Parenting
Dilemmas

Over the past 10 years in my current position as a school counselor in a K-8 school, I have written nearly 200 articles for our parent newsletter. It has been a luxury to share some of my opinions, disseminate research, and summarize work by professionals who have inspired me through their writings or in person. Much of what I write stems from situations which arise regularly in relationship with my students and their families. Some of it is deeply personal. All of it is my take on this Greatness Objective: How do we step fully and fearlessly into the greatest role of our lives? Each day is a challenge and different and surprising. Each connection we have with our children can be at once awe-inspiring and frightening, amusing and overwhelming. Our kids keep us up at night, even when they are sleeping. We carry them with us in our thoughts and prayers and in conversations and stories shared throughout the day. The great reward we work toward as parents is a lifetime relationship with someone who eventually becomes a self-aware adult, whom we hope hangs onto the lessons we have worked so hard to instill. I admit the ideas I share are biased, generally based on my background as a Nurtured Heart practitioner, and all based on my years of working with children. Feel free to copy and share as it fits your needs. Skip over, debate, or even rip out. You are the one who is in charge of this great role and roller coaster, and what a great and wild ride to Greatness it promises to be!

FEARLESS PARENTING ARTICLE TITLES

1. **An Argument for Arguing**

2. **A Lesson on Omission of the Truth Versus Lying**

3. **Everything We Do Is "Graded"**

4. **Giving Up Resentments**

5. **Giving Yourself Permission to Be Patient**

6. **The Output Often Mirrors the Input: My Lesson Learned**

7. **Is Your Kid Terrific? Take This Quiz.**

8. **Words to Live By**

9. **Silence is an Oxymoron**

10. **On Staying Present**

1. An Argument for Arguing

Arg!! Why can't I get my kid to stop arguing with me? Why must they challenge every simple request?? I have heard this lament many times. Oh, I think it was out of my own mouth! What does an arguing kid mean? That they don't respect our authority? That they don't like our rules? That they want power and choice? That they feel we are dictators of their freedom and choice? And how can I prepare him or her to handle authority figures in life if they are arguing with every rule and guideline? Certainly that is one way to approach the challenge. But what if I viewed it from a different lens? What could possibly be going right when my child has to argue over every single request I present? What does an arguing kid represent?

Imagine for a second, a child who completed every task you requested, who never made an excuse or whined about fairness and balance, who never pushed back or challenged your ideas and goals? At first, that sounds like a pretty lovely picture. Ah, peace. No more battles. Easy street. Now, imagine that child as a teen working with a dogmatic teacher, fearful to challenge an idea presented in her social justice class. Imagine that complacent child in her first relationship, not asking for what she needs, not setting her own limits or boundaries. Imagine that child as an adult employee lacking the confidence to assert her ideas or beliefs. And then as a parent, unwilling to set boundaries with her children! Yes, it is a leap, I know. But an arguing child is one who IS assertive, sees herself as powerful, able, and willing to challenge ideas, a deeper thinker and strong negotiator. An arguing child is one who analyzes ideas, who works to go beyond status quo, to understand and push you to an alternative perspective. An arguing child believes in his/her own potential, takes risks, and is a creative thinker. To me, this seems like a much preferred alternative to a "Yes, ma'am" in a world with bullies and targets.

That said, how WE respond to the argument remains critical. While we can take this paradigm shift in our vision of our arguing child, we know that our rules and guidelines exist purposefully to build capacity in our children, to be a part of a family, take responsibility, and develop skills that carry them into their future. Don't bother to explain this concept to your arguing children in the middle of the battle zone. But DO choose to remain calm, name their greatness (persistence, intelligence, assertiveness, high-level thinking), and remain firm. If your rules are sound, then there is no need to explain them ONCE MORE. No need to justify your logic nor belittle him/her. Remain firm, calm, and consistent. Because your children CAN handle it. And so can you. When you feel yourself heading down the slippery slope of anger, defensiveness, and frustration, <u>step away</u>. You are taking their resistance to your rule personally. Your job, remember, is to set boundaries, and their job is to test them. Look! You are both doing your job. Way to go!

"Yes, I know it is challenging." (Acknowledge feelings.) *"I know you can figure out how to get it done."* (Empowerment and capability.) *"You always impress me with your deep analysis and ability to push through even when you are frustrated."* (Naming capacity but being genuine.) And then,

this is critical: WALK AWAY. Once both parent and child are calmer, it is easy to restate the above once more. Lectures on why you have rules is really energy to the wrong person (Rules about YOU versus energy about YOUR CHILD'S ABILITY to be responsible, handle challenges, problem-solve, be a team player, etc.) They are honored and you remain positive, with no energy to the argument, just to the qualities of greatness in a "debater." I think that alone is worth the ARGUMENT.

2. A Lesson on Omission of the Truth Versus Lying

Probably one of the hardest dilemmas a parent confronts is lying. Let's just put this out there: All kids lie. It is as though they are hardwired for this. The level of severity of the lie is challenging because while we want to be "Strictness to Rules" (a.k.a. NO LYING), the world of a lie is often grey versus black and white. Is there a difference between not telling the truth and lying? You can see this would require a hearty debate, and one I love to have with my students over different examples. For the sake of this conversation, I simply want you to consider the idea that Strictness to Rules involves being very clear and transparent with the rules and the intention of the rules. Most kids lie for several reasons, and those reasons are the same ones for adults: 1) to get out of trouble, 2) out of fear of not being loved or disappointing someone, 3) to save face/social embarrassment. Additionally, well-intentioned adults often increase the opportunity for lying by using a system of interrogation that calls for self-preservation. I am remembering an exchange I had many years ago with two first graders prior to this insight. The supervisor had brought the two into the office. Cindy was crying and holding her cheek. Evan, the boy, was looking guilty, but tear-free.

"Did you hit Cindy?"

"She hit me!"

"How did she hit YOU?"

"Well, not on purpose."

"How do you hit someone not on purpose?"

"She ran into my hand when I was swinging it around."

Even as I recall this, it is hard not to chuckle. The urge to twist the full story to avoid blame comes frequently from not wanting to be seen as "bad." If you approach difficult moments like sibling fighting, with an assumption of shared responsibility, and you take away the shame, it becomes much easier for the perpetrator(s) to own behavior because they are so quickly reset. Pathological behaviors aside, much of the choices kids make are not always well-reasoned. If we approach children with the assumption that they are great, just not perfect, we once again make it safe for them to own up. We don't remove love. We increase love. We go into the conversation assuming each participant is culpable in someway, and we focus on the solution. Cindy is crying. How she got there is not nearly as important as repairing the situation. Cindy did not hit herself. Evan was accused. If we can give Evan a chance to restore his ego, he learns that it is safe to take ownership, and he can do some action of restorative justice to get him back on that Greatness Pedestal that he so badly wants to stay on. That's why he chose an omission of truth versus acceptance of responsibility. What happens now:

> *"Ouch. Looks like that hurts, Cindy. You both must have had a bit of a scuffle out there. I bet you are disappointed to be missing your recess, huh, Evan? I think you could be helpful and take Cindy down to the nurse. Can you do that for her?"*

Relieved, "Yeah..."

I hear him mumble as he walks out, "Sorry, Cindy."

The alternative parenting moment assumes guilt, but doesn't assume blame. Because we do not interrogate for who is to blame, but we assume an action occurred, we don't set anyone up to lie in a way protect his/her ego or get out of "trouble." Rather, we can set the guilty person up for accepting responsibility and making amends. We can set up our children for quick resets and opportunities to try again on their Greatness Pedestal. Isn't that what we want to happen anyway? It is mercy and reparation at its best.

3. Everything We Do Is "Graded"

On my first class day with my seventh graders in Personal and Social Development, I give them a quiz about the class expectations that they have just read silently. Inevitably, a core question is asked when these tasks are presented to motivated or frightened students, *"Will this be graded?"* Initially, I ignored the query. It was repeated and I forged ahead. After the simple quiz was done, I shared a concept that governs a bit of why I am careful with words and actions. "Everything we DO is graded," I responded to the students. "Every single thing we say, do, don't say, or don't do." I went on to give examples. "In class, when you blurt out: Graded. In the hallway, when you purposely bump a person: Graded. On the playground when you invite a loner to join in: Graded. In the lunchroom, when you make fun of an adult: Graded. At home on your computer, when you post a derogatory comment on your Facebook page: Graded. At a party, when you silently judge someone: Graded. On your sports team, when you push yourself hard in practice: Graded. Sure, it's not a letter grade. You aren't getting a 3.5 on self-control or a 2.0 on ethical behavior; however, I want you to understand how powerful your choices are in forming your character and connecting you to others." The old saying that actions speak louder than words can be equalized always by what we choose to say or not say, do or not do. We are 100 percent responsible for the words out of our mouths and all of our actions – and helping my students understand the impact of these actions seems to click when we talk about "grades."

Most of us are old enough to remember the days of pre-computer grading, when our teacher would give us a grade on our Citizenship. As we aim for the "S+" versus a "U" in the behavior and words of our children, it is important to consider who we are as models to our kids. How are we communicating with and about others? How open and tolerant are we to differences and changes? If we have concerns, do we go to the appropriate person directly or talk behind his/her back? Ironically, these choices are absorbed by our children, graded, and then, because we are their primary teacher, repeated. It is a powerful discussion to have with your child. Considering the impact (grade) of our actions.

As I collected their quizzes, not actually giving a letter grade, to many a student's relief, I reminded them that the most powerful grade they earn in life is who they are in relationship to others. "Build relationship and be the kind of person with whom others seek to do the same" is the gist of what I impress upon my students. Everything else is just a letter grade that most won't remember years to come. They will remember who you are and how you treat and speak of others. A *Greatness Grade* of sorts, I guess. At the playground, classroom, dinner table, even in the line at Starbucks, here is to earning high marks all year long.

4. Giving Up Resentments

Last year, my own parent disappointed me by forgetting a birthday. Last month, I felt slighted by a co-worker. Last week, a friend hurt my feelings with a sarcastic comment. Yesterday, I once again had to do a chore that I had asked my daughter to do. Frustrating? Disappointing? Common? Sure, but so much of our stories of resentment fall into what is going wrong and harboring bad feelings because of that misdemeanor. A resentment is a grudge that you harbor after you've felt mistreated. It's easy to hold on to all the incidents that angered you, from a gossiping parent to a sarcastic co-worker to a forgetful spouse. Dr. Judith Orloff, author of a wonderful read called *Emotional Freedom* (c. 2009), shares that "*...if you took a poll, you'd probably get a lot of people on your side about your right to stay resentful. According to such logic, as time passes, you have 'the right' to get angrier, becoming a broken record of complaints.*" And I suppose you might. But is this how you want to frame your world, your relationships, your world, and your focus?

Having spent many hours talking parents, teachers, students, and friends, off the proverbial cliff of angry resentment, I have realized how much freedom really does come from letting go. So you may be right about being wronged. So what? I teach my students regularly that while we can't change people, we are in control of our own response to them. We can learn and we can be powerful in that learning. We can let someone know that they disappointed us, let us down, made us angry. Then it is up to them to decide if reparation is part of their plan. And up to

US to let it go, regardless; up to US to shift our energy and focus and to forgive without expectation.

I often recall a story of a seventh grader who, while trouble-shooting a conflict with a peer, said to me, "Well, back in kindergarten, XXX (the student he was angry with) did YYY (some past action)." Wow! Seven years of deep resentment. Seven years of emotional power given to someone else, instead of renewed in forgiveness. So many hours lost on negative energy directed at a past incident. So many lost moments of joy.

Dr. Orloff refers to resentments like *"dragging dead bodies around."* Sorry about that gruesome analogy, but I find it to be a strong, visual reminder of the burden resentment can create in our psyche.

"Forgiveness is a state of grace, nothing you can force or pretend," Orloff states eloquently. "Forgiveness penetrates the impenetrable — the obstinacy that stifles love, the tenacious pain that dams our energy reserves. A Stanford research study showed that forgiveness significantly decreases stress, rage and psychosomatic symptoms. I'm not saying that betrayal is ever justified, that you aren't entitled to be upset if someone wrongs you, or that you shouldn't try to improve or else leave a destructive situation." (www.drjudithorloff.com) That is healthy self-care. However, forgiveness goes beyond the act and is directed at the person: the offender, rather than the offense. And in the long run, those hurt the most by resentment tend to be ourselves.

Howard Glasser, creator of the Nurtured Heart Approach mirrors this thinking when he talks about energy to negativity. Resentment stops you short and focuses you on the problem (negativity). Resentment keeps you in the past and makes the future murky. Forgiveness empowers relationships, models greatness, and moves us to a future where we learn from our past, but don't live in it. Here is to some deep thinking, and ready forgiveness ahead.

5. Giving Yourself Permission to be Patient

Wait a minute. Be patient. Hold on a sec. Just a moment. I'll be right with you. Can you hold? Thanks for your patience. Just recently I became aware of how often the quality of patience was required daily. There are so many things that require us to wait. The traffic light, the carpool driver, the child who can't find her other shoe, the co-worker who needs to do one more thing, the instructor who keeps repeating himself, the person in the line in front of us who forgot one item, the child who begins a conversation and can't remember all the details (and details are what they want to tell you when you, impatiently, want just the "gist"). A recent long bout of early snowfall in the Northwest was a real test for many working to tap into our Inner Patience. We waited for snow. We waited for power. We waited for Internet and phone and school to get back in session. Many people are very good at this. Remarkably good, in fact. Rather than digress to a list of ways to be patient, ways to teach patience, or reasons to be patient, I thought I might consider first, why we are impatient to begin with – and then perhaps, by this self-awareness we can shift to become, if not gifted at patience, at least a bit more patient with our attempts.

So here are some of the common mindsets of the impatient:

1. *I need it now.*
2. *I am always in a hurry.*
3. *Other people's expectations make me impatient.*
4. *I hate wasting time.*

5. *I don't like to wait for things/people that I shouldn't have to wait for.*

6. *I need to be in control.*

You can see the trouble we get into when we are the role models of patience for our children. We make quick judgments, rather than think through the consequences or choices. We purchase (and eat) hastily. We drive too fast. We honk our horns. We react rather than respond. We complain. We snap at people – strangers at best, our loved ones at worst. We settle for less and we harbor resentment. We are never our best selves when we are impatient. And ironically most of us have little patience for impatient people!

As we consider our year ahead, one that promises some interesting political and economical challenges, it seems a good time to focus on what we do have control over. Take a minute (oh, that means you gotta be patient with yourself yet again), and consider who in your world, today, could use more of YOUR patience. Recognize which mindset governs most of your impatient responses and then consider some of these Truths of the Patient:

1. *You eventually get what you want most of the time.*

2. *Your ability to be patient sets the tone for everyone you are with at the time.*

3. *What really matters most is people.*

4. *And the things that do really matter, often take more time.*

5. *Life is the marathon; be in it for the long haul (which always takes patience) versus the sprint of the moment.*

6. *The only thing we can truly control in our world is our attitude.*

Why not name this the Year of the Patient Parent/Co-Worker/Friend/Partner/Stranger. Set a goal for yourself. Make it a NOW goal but be (wait for it ☺) **patient** with yourself if it takes a while to break an old mindset. It's good to idle at the red light and recognize we can.

6. The Output Often Mirrors the Input: My Lesson Learned

(Author Warning: *Heavy Bias Ahead*)

"No parking or waiting on the Airport Drive," my daughter blurted randomly one evening as I was preparing dinner. She was two-and-a-half years old. This situation had obviously burned itself in my memory (as she is now nearly 18 years old), and I recall turning to my husband (to whom she had been entrusted previously that day), "So I take it you were at the airport this afternoon?" I asked rhetorically. We laughed. He had waited (despite the obvious warning) on that dang Airport Drive, to pick up a client and drive him (with toddler in tow) to his hotel. The story remains a stand out in my mind, as I am confronted repeatedly with children who see and know more than their developmental brains and young life experience should be exposed to. Our children not only hear what we say, they remember what they hear. They, in fact, pay more attention to their surroundings more often than we do. Downloaded to the Tabula Rasa, their open minds that sponge it all in. Lesson learned by my husband. Lesson transferred to me.

The world our kids are exposed to today is hugely more "adult" than the world we navigated ourselves. Even the Cartoon Network has slipped off its Greatness Pedestal with the incorporation of adult themes, jokes, and messages. We know the risk of this begins with the uncomfortable question and multiplies with the age-inappropriate behavior. How DO we help our kids REMAIN kids for as long as possible?

Under the same vein as Santa and the Easter Bunny, I coach my younger students repeatedly to "Take their time being a kid. We adults are tired of being adults. You are only a kid for so long. Adulthood, man, its forever!!" But despite my message, the media, the music, the access to violent video games, and suggestive programs, put our children at risk of skipping the best days we remember. Childhood should be about fantasy (our children's own imagination, not some video reality). It should be about friendship (face to face, not online gaming partners or texting blurbs). It should be about being physical and pushing our young, capable bodies (not sitting in front of a screen playing a game or opting for a chat versus a spontaneous game of capture the flag).

We get this as parents, I believe. We have a screen. That wonderful pre-frontal lobe, which makes some generally fabulous executive functioning decisions in regards to risk-assessment and goal planning, is well tuned. Our kids? Not so much. Now, more than ever, we are needed as parents. It isn't the "Are they going to play with matches!" or "Don't play in the street!" that becomes a fear. It is a stark reality that our kids aren't playing physically enough; that they have sideline and direct exposure to adult-themed materials. Kids aren't different; they remain sponges who download whatever they are exposed to – and then try to make sense of it at their limited developmental stage. Our world is. There are few restrictions on media. Cartoons are not just for kids. Adult shows with challenging scenes, dialogue, vocabulary, and situations run all day long – rather than at the after 9 p.m. rule that most grew up experiencing. We are not going to change this new reality – and actually being critical or spending energy bemoaning the changes won't make us great either.

With the possibility that perhaps your child has downloaded some confusing information about life, relationships, bodies, and her/his world, what then? My gut leans toward *developmental* honesty. Our bodies are not shameful. Men and women in relationships is natural. Curiosity about all the messages is also natural. So as awkward as these conversations might be, power on courageously. Remember, they "know" or have ideas beyond anything you really thought you knew at their age. Ask. Respond. Keep it simple but honest. "I will tell you when you are older," really will not buy you what you are seeking (more childhood for your child). Simple, non-emotional explanations will reduce anxiety and curiosity for them. And the great thing is that, at early ages, distraction still works! Use movies and cartoons to help them begin to understand relationships first. Don't stop trying to understand them yourself!

Then continue to pay attention to what they pay attention to, also. My principal and I have had so many stories shared by parents of late. "I don't know where he learned that." "We don't talk like that at home." Of course not – and yes, your little sponge hears all, sees all, wants all. So when it the output mimics inappropriate words or actions, the "how did he/she learn that?" is significantly less relevant than how you respond. Keep your anger and surprise private. Be present in that moment and fearless in setting the boundary. Those words are used often as a test, and frequently without the understanding of their offensive nature. They are seeking reaction. Keep yours neutral and firm. Remove the energetic response of shock or lecturing. Keep it simple and clear. "We absolutely do not use words (actions) like that. It hurts others and makes others uncomfortable." Remove them from relationship. The opportunity for education around the right choices comes before the misstep and afterwards. Using media that is appropriate and stories that are age-relevant. Tap into his/her own experiences of being uncomfortable, embarrassed, confused, and hurt. Be available to educate what words and actions really mean or imply.

The actions of grabbing another child's private body parts or getting overly physical are often also early mimicked behaviors. Television and games are not the only culprits. They admire older kids. They admire adults. You can likely recall this feeling from your own youth. All kids want to be older. With age, comes responsibility. With youth, comes freedom. My kid was on that darn "Airport Drive" for too long, obviously (her dad confessed that it was over 20 minutes – thus the download!), but he, too, was caught unaware of that "white noise" that becomes the words and ideas owned and tested by a developing brain. Guess this is a simple reminder to monitor, adjust, and pay attention to the words you say and the visuals you watch. Be the diligent parent and consider this: It ain't Big Brother watching. It's your child. Always.

7. Is Your Kid Terrific? Take this Quiz.

I recently clipped a newspaper editorial written by syndicated columnist, John Rosemond, one of my favorite child psychologists and authors, and chuckled at its perspective. The ironic title (above) intrigued me. Rosemond (www.rosemond.com) commented on the frequent bumper sticker sighting, *"My Child Is A Terrific Kid,"* which comes from some character-building curriculum taught in many schools. One wonders, *"What parent doesn't think his/her kid is terrific?"* The actual system of student recognition, which is rewarded with the coveted bumper sticker, is amusingly modified a bit by Rosemond with his version of a *"15-item inventory that will tell parents whether their child is truly terrific or not, and if not, needs some work....A child begins with 15 points. Deduct one point for every item that is not almost always true. A child who ends up with 14 or 15 points is a Truly Terrific Kid. A child who scores 11 to 13 means the child is sort of terrific; 9 to 10 reflects less than terrific; and 8 or below is not terrific."* Gulp. Some of the graded items continue toward impossible: *"#1 Eats whatever food is served without complaint. #2 Does his homework without being told...#4-5 are about manners, #9 Neither creates nor participates in conflicts with or between peers (#13 is between siblings), #12 Goes to bed in his own bed without complaint and goes quickly to sleep, #14 Accepts responsibility when confronted with misdeeds"*... and so it goes. I am sure all our children are well on their way to earning the **Terrific Kid** sticker.

Kidding aside, it seems we do look to honor kids often for their good choices and behaviors. But sometimes, I believe, the true credit for these good choices should go more often to that dedicated parent who consistently held high expectations, provided boundaries and support, taught initial skills, and put in the hard work from the beginning.

With Mother's Day upon us, and being a biased mother myself, I am thinking the new sticker prize should say, "**My Parent Is a Terrific Parent**" and could appear on the child's backpack, bike helmet (because, of course, who taught them to wear one), homework folder, washed clothing, award certificate, and team sports equipment. Ours would be a scale TOO monumental to measure and may contain some of the following:

The Terrific Parent....

1. Ensures that her family is generally fed regularly and healthfully, including all the pets.

2. Organizes the house so that most things can be found eventually, and most things washed, eventually.

3. Admires profusely the artwork and projects of his child, especially the handmade cards and gifts he is to display and dutifully find useful.

4. Avoids swearing in FRONT of her kids if at all possible. But she may be forgiven when she trips on the shoes that were left, yet again, in the same spot where her son

left them the last time she asked him to put them in the bin.

5. Drives willingly to school, soccer, volleyball, track, scouts, Tae Kwan Do, youth group, bake sales, last-minute runs to the Staples store for the poster board for the book report/special person/science project that your daughter thought she told you about (except you weren't in the room when she told you).

6. Intervenes in escalating battles between siblings without whining herself.

7. Provides unconditional love even when he feels overwhelmed and unappreciated.

8. Gives up sleep to mend wounds, calm fears, help with homework, make lunches, and wait up to ensure curfew is met.

9. Recognizes, and goes out of her way to name, all the good choices her child makes each day even when it is hard – or she is tired – because the curfew was at midnight.

10. Rewards good choices, and does not back down from holding his child to the rules and expectations because he KNOWS he is capable.

11. Walks the dog that he didn't want to get in the first place, because he knew he would be the one walking him.

12. Offers hugs freely and tries not to get her feelings hurt when she no longer gets to kiss her child goodbye when she drops him off at school.

And so our list would go.

Of course, our kids are terrific. But let's remember whom we can credit for doing much of the hard work and making it look easy: A MOM! A DAD! A Day? Just one day to honor each??? Bring on the bumper stickers. I am voting for *every* day to be Mother's and Father's Day. Of course, this could get out of hand when I start to get on my soapbox and ponder the sainthood of teachers next!

8. Words to Live By

Certainly a phrase we toss around. Do unto others. Don't procrastinate. Set goals. Forgive easily. Help others. In my eighth grade Personal and Social Development class, I ask students to come up with their own motto. What do you want to stand for? Their words to live by are powerful phrases of their sure future. If they have owned the positive words that others have shared about them, then their goal and personal motto is one that is fearless and inspiring. Words are so powerful. Like the old saying of sticks and stones breaking bones, each of my students recognize so clearly that words are actually at the core of healing and hurting much more powerfully than a stone or a Band-Aid. Words are what we remember.

When I coach parents in my monthly parent group or train teachers across the state, I tackle this issue head on. The power of our voice and the messages we give and receive can be irrevocable. Nearly everyone can recall the words said by a teacher or adult mentor/parent from their youth. Words have the power to transform (*"You are a gifted thinker with such insight."*). Or destroy (*"You are always such a naughty girl!"*). With words, we can build up or take down, add value or diminish. This concept works in our favor when it comes to written contracts, but is so damaging when it comes to people. We depend on words for our relationships; they are the big bucks in sales, and the clincher in love. (What would Hallmark do without words?) But what words do we dole out to our kids each day? What words do we take in? What words do we scold ourselves with in our heads, when we, yet again, forget to pick up the dry cleaning on the way home or leave the signed permission slip on the counter? We can be brutal to ourselves and then, in turn, use those same words with the deadly dagger of sarcasm to do real damage to others. In our writing or sound bites (for youth texting), we can be misunderstood quite easily, because there is no tone, even with a smiley face emoticon. ☹ So, as role models to our children, we need to be diligent about the words we use and live by. Do we keep our word? Do we build up our children's capacity to handle the world with our words? Do we rescue kids from consequences with our words and then build in them a weakness that depletes? Or do we use our words to hold them positively accountable? Our words can remind them they are greatly made and greatly capable.

When I lead discussions with students in class meetings, we debunk the phrase, "Just kidding" as a poor-man's apology. "If you have to follow any statement with the words, 'just kidding', then likely you have just said something purposely hurtful," I point out. And while sarcasm is the fodder for most television comedy, it is the destroyer of trust and relationship when used without caution or a screen. Along this similar vein, I know very few who claim they like to hang out with negative people. And when I ask them what makes a person negative, they will often name the words they use. Negative people complain. They focus on what is wrong with work, kids, teachers, traffic, weather, in-laws. They whine. They nag. But positive people? They see the world as abundance and potential. Positive people use words to name greatness, to recognize good choices and then to build more of those. They laugh more easily at themselves and accept the challenges of life as capacity-building. They tell jokes which are not at the expense of others. They are not generally sarcastic. But they may be self-deprecating because they know down deep, that they are great. Positive people get the power of words and choose carefully. They receive only what empowers them; and in turn, use words to name those gifts in others. Positive people get that we all live by words and they purposely use words to live by. Such a good opportunity to consider what words will you choose to be known for.

9. Silence Is an Oxymoron

One summer recently, I had throat surgery to remove some polyps on my vocal folds. For five days, I was instructed to not talk, to not even whisper. (I guess that is even harder on your vocal cords.) During those days, I had some insights on this idea of silence, and I rediscovered its best gift: LISTENING. As I was home sick two days following with strep throat, I once again revisited this concept. Blessed and blessings, in disguise.

A funny thing happens when you lose your ability to talk. You listen. You listen a lot more. Each word you push to say hurts or requires huge effort, and so you choose each word with great care. You pare it down. You mull it over in your head, honing your vocabulary to make sure the play of sounds is correct. You avoid soft verbs for vibrant ones; you slide over trite adjectives and use some less familiar words like pretentious, spurious, and cathartic (not in the same sentence).

I have been mute for just five days and it has been a test of generous will. To think but to not speak? Wow. (How many politicians in our world could learn from vocal folds surgery?) While I jest about the silence of my voice, I have come to learn that silence is not an authentic reality. Our brains are never quiet. There is never real stillness in any room, even as you try to drift off to sleep. You exchange the hum of the fan, the bark of distant dogs or sirens, for the active, eager brain that waits to leap into action, convoluting your experiences into unreal options and bizarre stories that make Harry Potter look possible. Silence, I realize, is a symbolic word only. It does not ever exist. Do you listen silently? Heck no! Your thoughts begin arguing, defending, absorbing, or calculating every idea tossed your way. Even in silence, we engage advertisement that mindlessly plays on the radio, the background conversation of a couple in the grocery line, the sermon at church, the lecture from a parent. In fact, silence, in and of itself, can still mean something significant. When we talk, we have <u>intention</u> of meaning. When we are silent, with the exception of the true mute, it is always a choice. Even I could talk; however, I was advised if I wanted to get better, I should not. How often have we all wanted to speak, but held our tongues. Or wanted someone else to speak up, but they didn't. In these moments, silence speaks loudly. Here is our oxymoron.

Still, in the stillness of words, we can't seem to shut off the monologue. Stillness is something I thought I craved until I realized it was nonexistent. Silence, I heard said simply, is the absence of sound. And many of us have heard it called *golden*. Scientifically, I imagine there actually might be this real phenomenon: an absence of sound in space. But I have yet to hear it here on earth. What about golden? Having dabbled in the world of the mute this past week, I would say I may agree with that description. The ability, and eventually, the choice not to speak, allowed me a different window into my world. Silent is not a world I have occupied, nor have most of those around me. In fact, I have been accused of being loud all my life. I live loudly. I talk loudly. I opinionate loudly. And now I get to hear what I sound like.

I guess I just get to smile a bit at the arrogance of words and the wisdom of silence. Words are big and often empty in platitudes. Words puff themselves around people and ideas without often considering the audience buy-in. They are nervous energy and sap the space of silence. In the same way a swear word sounds awkward and wrong coming from the mouth of a teenager, many words spoken without the time to think about all the sides of the multifaceted world sound spurious (aha!). The talent for using words best lies with the poet, the true minimalist of words. And the thing about a poem is that it takes a commitment to read one. You have to decide to engage in the idea created. You have to be open to hearing a different view and a different way of saying something. The poet gets it. Words are precious. Choose carefully. Choose again. Wait. Silence. Pause. Breathe.

Now, as I began to dabble once again into spoken words, I find that I capitalize on my muteness and default to listening, eavesdropping, waiting, nodding, and encouraging talking. Perhaps you only get so many words in life. Perhaps that is the measure of a life: Your words. And when you use them up – that's it. Silence. Real silence. Hear that? Shhh... Someone is thinking right now.

10. On Staying Present

Let's just call it as we know it: Parenting is stressful. When we are with our children, we are generally more tense and alert. We are cautious and concerned about the choices they make, the schedule they follow, the food they eat or don't eat, they way they act around other kids and adults. We worry. We plan. We avoid, and we structure. We diagnose and predict and hyper focus, so absorbed are we in their struggles and successes. It is always interesting to look back on a quick year of a child's life and wonder how it sped by. Were we not just celebrating his seventh birthday last month and now he is eight? And when our children are infants, despite our deep, dear "head-over-heels-never-been-this-in-love-before" feeling, we also long for future days when our children might be more independent, sleep more, demand less.

As a veteran mom of advancing-in-age teenagers, I was listening to the radio as I was driving without them one day. (Not Raffi or Disney or rap music or pop hits, but music of my own choice. This is a luxury you DO get back when you are not driving with your children.) A song by Darius Rucker came on, and the lyrics stung with their accuracy. "Your gonna miss this one day," he sings as he tells the journey of life with his daughter rushing in her world to the next moment of her life (marriage, bigger houses, babies, etc.). In the sleep-deprived moment, when your children won't stop bickering, when every toy you just put away is pulled out again, when your child gets in his first trike/bike/skate/car accident, you wish time to speed ahead from this moment to one which appears easier. His song was a sobering reminder to me of how many times I wasn't in the present, savoring the challenge and the opportunity of being the Queen of Problem Solving to my child.

In Tina Fey's hit book *Bossypants* (c. 2011), she writes a mock letter to her now five-year-old daughter, bringing her full circle to appreciating her mother for all she did for her during those early baby years. Tina does this as she describes a future daughter taking care of her own exhausting, but worthy baby. It is the circle of life, to quote one of the best Disney flicks created, *The Lion King*, but sometimes it carries you like a whirlpool, leaving you amazed at its tenacity. Nothing stays the same. Nothing can be repeated. Sometimes we are so busy with our life of raising kids, we miss the idea that even the happiest of times will be short-lived. The hardest and saddest will also fade. Nothing stays. Waxing deeply philosophical here, I am simply going to suggest that accepting where you are now and APPRECIATING the moment is critical in your role as parent and partner.

I can remember when my first daughter was a colicky infant of many weeks. Deeply in love with her, I also felt ill-equipped to solve whatever made her little body unhappy. When she was finally still, she was so lovely and precious. And I was exhausted. She would resist sleep, and like many other colicky babies, the evening hours were long and loud. I kept wondering when life would get back to "normal." When would I get more sleep? When would I know what to expect and have a routine, as I had had in my months and years prior? Every morning felt new and hopeful, because she was more content then, rewarding my deprivation. It was one of these mornings, as I was nursing her and staring numbly at old reruns of *Little House on the Prairie,* that it finally dawned on me: THIS is the new normal, this life without complete control or routine or structure. This life with another life that is not mine, but which I am responsible for, is now the <u>new</u> normal. There was no going back. There was only this moment and the next and the next.

Glasser, in his book *Transforming the Difficult Child,* highlights this fact when he coaches parents to look through a lens of success and capture the next moment, naming and honoring what you see your child doing, and not doing. This idea of staying present means we do not go back to past mistakes and harp on them. We do not bring up errors and hold them up as examples of what <u>not</u> to do. We look at now. We energize what is right now. We stay present and we stay ready.

I had not read Glasser's work yet; he was not published. (Man, could he have saved me some wasted energy on the past, whoops, like now. Reset.) But in that moment of awareness, as I nursed my first daughter, I began to recognize the preciousness of time. Likely, I was too sleep-deprived to really absorb it all.

When you are pregnant or expecting a child, you focus on the baby. You think about baby things. You pay attention to other people's babies and notice pregnant women much more often. Very few of us spend energy on seeing our baby as a teenager or a college student or a fifth grader. We can't even picture what our baby will look like. It is one of our most present moments in parenting. We pay attention to the NOW.

Staying present means we do not foreshadow our relationship beyond the moment of each interaction. Each interaction has the potential to set our children up for this future we desire for them, making them capable to handle all the challenges of life. But it is in the moment of NOW that matters.

If you have ever gone on a long road trip with small children, you likely have discovered that children have little sense of the passage or concept time. "How much longer?" they whine. And then, just 30 minutes later, they query again. A planned birthday party can be just about too much for their little systems to manage. It could be two weeks from now yet they wake each day asking if it is today. A big family trip to Disneyland could be months from now, and they wonder when you are leaving. Time has no relevancy to children. Keeping this developmental fact in mind can provide us with our own window into living in the now, as our children do.

In coaching parents, I find that many come to me with fears of the future for their children. What if they can't learn to listen? What if they never get organized? What will happen if they don't do their homework? How will they turn out okay in our split family? What if they never learn to take responsibility? What can their possible future be if they never tell the truth? Heartfelt fears often drive parenting responses. Yet this type of future-based thinking can prevent us from living in the now and recognizing the good choices our kids make all the time. Like right now, as you are reading this, what might you be able to say about the great choices your child made today? Simple things that keep us forward-moving but present living, make some of the best parenting opportunities. Eating breakfast without complaint. Expressing an opinion without yelling. Listening without interrupting. Turning off the electronics even when they didn't want to. Laughing at your jokes. Helping her little sister. Buckling his own seatbelt. Waiting patiently until you were off the phone to ask a question. (This last is still something I am waiting to energize with my teenagers!) Doing the hard thing even when it is hard.

If we can remind ourselves to live in the now, this moment, instead of looking to the future, we can give our kids the gift of a present US.

APPENDICES

1. **Resources and References**
2. **More about Kids At Hope™**
3. **Words of Greatness (A Beginner's Adjective List)**

1. Resources and References

Throughout this book, I have referenced several authors, presenters, and contributors. In most cases, I cite directly in context. Here are some of the core references for future exploration.

NURTURED HEART APPROACH:

Transforming the Difficult Child: The Nurtured Heart Approach, by Howard Glasser & Jennifer Easley (2003)

The Inner Wealth Initiative: The Nurtured Heart Approach for Educators, by Tom Grove and Howard Glasser, (2007)

Transforming the Difficult Child Workbook: An Interactive Guide to the Nurtured Heart Approach, by Howard Glasser, Joann Bowdidge, and Lisa Bravo (2008)

All Children Flourishing: Igniting the Greatness of Our Children The Nurtured Heart Approach – a Parenting Paradigm for the New Millennium, by Howard Glasser (2008)

Transforming the Difficult Child: True Stories of Triumph, edited by Jennifer Easley and Howard Glasser (2009) (A story of mine appears on p57–59)

There Is Always Something Going Right: Workbook for Implementing the Nurtured Heart Approach in School Settings, by Tammy Small and Louisa Triandis (2010)

Notching Up the Nurtured Heart Approach: The New Inner Wealth Initiative for Educators, by Howard Glasser and Melissa Lynn Block (2011) *

(*Note: Chart mentioned in Chapter 5 can be found on page 120; reference to a workshop participant's feedback of mine is given on page 139)

Articles and other information can be found on my website at www.nurturedheart.net. For more information on the Nurtured Heart Approach visit www.ChildrensSuccessFoundation.com.

OTHER BOOKS REFERENCED:

You Are a Social Detective: Explaining Social Thinking to Kids, by Michelle Garcia Winner and Pamela Cooke (2008) www.socialthinking.com

The Minds of Boys: Saving Our Sons from Falling Behind in School and Life, by Michael Gurian (2007) www.michaelgurian.com

Parent's Little Book of Lists: Do's & Don'ts of Effective Parenting, by Dr. Jane Bluestein (1997) www.janebluestein.com

Kids at Hope: Every Child Can Succeed, No Exceptions Book, by John P. Carlos and Rick Miller (2008)

Youth Development from the Trenches, by Rick Miller (2012)

Bossy Pants, by Tina Fey (2011)

Emotional Freedom: Liberate Yourself from Negative Emotions and Transform Your Life, by Judith Orloff, M.D. (2010)

Give Your Hearts Out to Everybody: Third Graders' Rules for Making the Right Choices at School by St. Anthony School 3rd Graders (2012)

More about Kids At Hope™

The culture of Kids at Hope (KAH) intersects directly with the social curriculum constructs of the Nurtured Heart Approach: *All Children Living in and for Their Greatness*

As part of KAH Northwest Leadership Team, I align them as follows:

Kids at Hope is a grassroots program designed to inspire, empower, and transform children from at risk to at hope. Using resources, core practices, a clear belief system and the power of significant adults in children's world, KAH establishes school, agency and citywide cultures where kids are successful – no exception.

Utilizing similar constructs and the significant role of adults in children's lives, the Nurtured Heart Approach is the tool/language-used/energy driven social curriculum that transforms students' characters and spirits, giving them a deep conviction that they can cope with problems and succeed socially and emotionally. NHA refers to this personal power as inner wealth.

The intention of this system of relationship is to bring out the best version of each person with whom we are in relationship: 1) By not leaking negative energy toward a child/individual's poor choices or behavior; 2) By flooding them with positive recognition, using a compass which points to what going right and going out of our way to always name it specifically; and 3) by keeping high expectations/strictness to rules: BECAUSE ALL CHILDREN ARE CAPABLE OF SUCCESS – No Exceptions!

The Belief Systems of *Kids at Hope* and *The Nurtured Heart Approach* intersect neatly on the above points. Both systems recognize the incredible potential of each child. They call significant adults to respond and help build this capacity in the way they speak, treat, and are in relationship with each child. They place clear, high expectations on a child, because the child is worthy of their greatness and capable of handling all the consequences of their choices.

The Nurtured Heart Approach can be adapted into the trainings of the significant adults working with youth (teachers, parents, playground staff, bus drivers, lunchroom monitors, instructional aids, specialists, administrators, front office staff, custodians, grandparents, etc.) by giving each adult the clear constructs of this communication. Many adults, because they care about kids, are misguided in the kind of recognition that is powerful and transforming. We use "good job" and "thank you" randomly, not understanding that the goal of KAH and NHA is "meaningful, sustainable" relationships. Positive recognition must be connected to irrefutable evidence of their greatness. The mentor for the ELL child must not just say "good job" to the completed task, but name the quality of greatness it took for that child to be successful. The skills of students to stay focused, persistent, organized, cooperative, responsible; these are the qualities that carry them into that attainable future which KAH names.

Secondly, NHA empowers adults to uphold high expectations and be firm and consistent with broken rules, because ALL CHILDREN ARE CAPABLE OF SUCCESS – No Exceptions! Therefore, NHA does not give warnings for broken rules. There is no "Next time you do that, you will lose a privilege," because the child can handle it. Whoops. Broke a rule. Lost that privilege. However, the powerful transition here, is that because both NHA and KAH have a belief system based on success, there is no energy given to the broken rule, the doling of the quick "time-out," etc. NO lectures, no warnings, no arguing, no threatening, no nagging. Simple, brief, energy-less response. Our ultimate goal is always TIME-IN to greatness and success. We, as significant adults, look for the quick rejoining back into the "game" and put our energy toward recognizing all that the child is doing well. Many caring and compassionate adults working with youth will try to make exceptions for broken rules. NHA helps them to realize that an exception can reconfirm to a child that they are not capable of following the rules or meeting the expectation. But they are capable, each one of them. No Exceptions!

Kids at Hope takes a positive reversal to a term that is problem-focused, "Kids at Risk," and reminds us that how we see kids is the first powerful step. Therefore, it is absolutely essential that our lens is constantly aiming on what is right. And, there is always something right to be named! The child forgot his pencil. But he is on time. She pushed another student. But she was honest in that moment. Our ultimate goal is to bring a child quickly back toward his/her greatness.

As adults naming the greatness, we can help a child to see his/her own capacity and scaffold them back onto that stand as quickly as possible. We welcome them back quickly and with positive recognition of their self-control, responsibility and respect.

A *Nurtured Heart* practitioner takes 3 clear Stands: 1) Because you are great, I refuse to energize negativity with warnings, reminders, arguing, etc. 2) I refuse not to see you, and name whatever I see, as great and greatness. 3) and because you are capable of this greatness I will consequence each choice you make.

The Nurtured Heart Approach puts the child's capability back into the hand of the child, so that *Kids At Hope*™ gain the inner wealth to name and reach for that clear, attainable future.

Words of Greatness: A Beginner's Adjective List

By this behavior, you are
being/showing/demonstrating/are so...

LOYAL	THINKS AHEAD
TENACIOUS	HONEST
WELL-INTENTIONED	JOYFUL
	INTENSE
ASSERTIVE	EMPATHETIC
SUNNY	PATIENT
FRIENDLY	CARING
HILARIOUS	COOPERATIVE
FOCUSED	BRILLANT
COMPASSIONATE	QUICK LEARNER
KIND	CONSIDERATE
THOUGHTFUL	PLAYFUL
INQUISITIVE	FAIR NEGOTIATOR
GENEROUS	TALENTED
ARTICULATE	PERSISTENT
ENERGETIC	DETERMINED
CREATIVE	INTELLIGENT
GOOD WITH HANDS	ADVENTUROUS

PROBLEM-SOLVER

STRONG LISTENER

ORGANIZED

SELF-RESPONSIBLE

STRONG-WILLED

PERSISTENT

BEAUTIFUL

SPIRITED

DETAIL-ORIENTED

ETHICAL

TRUE TO FAITH

ANTICIPATES WELL

MATURE

BIG-HEARTED

RESPECTFUL

PASSIONATE

CLEVER

CHARMING

PEACEMAKER

ENGAGING

RESILIENT

COMMITTED

DEEP THINKER

FLEXIBLE

SELF-AWARE

FORGIVING

CALM

RESOURCEFUL

LOVING

SENSITIVE

CAREFUL

WISE

TOLERANT

TRUTHFUL

CHEERFUL

QUICK THINKER

COMPOSED

ATHLETIC

GOOD

COMMUNICATOR

DEMONSTRATES

INTEGRITY

FOLLOWS

DIRECTIONS